WHITEWATER

In B.C.'s Southwest

A Guide to Accessible Runs for Beginner to Advanced Kayakers

by

Steve Crowe & Jim Hnatiak

published by Steve Crowe
Kamloops, BC
2001

National Library of Canada Cataloguing in Publication Data

Crowe, Steve, 1969-
    Whitewater in B.C.'s southwest: a guide to accesible runs for beginner to
    advanced kayakers

ISBN 0-9688038-0-6

1. Kayaking—British Columbia—Lower Mainland—Guidebooks.
2. Lower Mainland (B.C.)—Guidebooks. I. Hnatiak, Jim 1968- II. Title.

GV776.15.B7C76 2001   797.1'224'097113   C2001-900114-2

Photo credits: all photos by Steve Crowe and Jim Hnatiak except pp 38, 43, 93 and 95
(Monica De), p 12 (Kevin Pearson), p 90 (Rick Hayes), p 104 {horizontal} (Colin Hunko)

Thanks

We thank Betty Pratt-Johnson for inspiration. Her book <u>Whitewater Trips: Greater Vancouver to Thompson River Region</u> guided us to many of the rivers we have paddled here. This began as just two guys who liked river running and camping. We picked up <u>Whitewater Trips</u> early in the game so that it could lead us to variety. As the years passed we began to notice the aging of the book: take-outs had become private, put-ins had disappeared, camping spots were charging, roads had changed, bridges built, etc. Desperate to avoid "real" work, we thought it would be fun to note these differences in the summer of 2000. Which ties into…

We also thank the Grand Canyon and the Colorado River that made it. We were extremely fortunate, also in the summer of 2000, to be invited to paddle this 18-day route. For this we want to thank Dave (House of the Flying Bandit) Couture and his imperturbable wife Rachel Workum. It is no small honor to be included on a Grand list because Dave waited 10 years for his private trip permit to come up. After ten years he had many candidates to choose from. Because we were invited in the spring and the trip was in August, we had plenty of foreknowledge. We knew we had to improve as we weren't as good as the Grand. And after 10 years of waiting you don't say 'no thanks, I'll get the next one'. So the only way to improve was to practice. Practice meant paddling on moving water. As we would have had to quit our jobs in August anyway, we quit them early, picked up a pen and notepad and went kayaking.

Thanks to paddlers. We want people to paddle these rivers. Sure overcrowding sucks, but people are power - more paddlers means more protective voices for the rivers. If we can get people from the United States to love our rivers as they are, perhaps they will be less inclined to dam and divert them to build more golf courses in the Mojave Desert. If we can get more locals to love their rivers, perhaps they will be less inclined to let the US control them. And, on a more philosophical note, it is always fun to watch beginners flounder.

And thanks to the following, in no particular order: Tom Fair, Darlene Christianson, Sherri King, Jamie McDonnell, Todd Thompson and Charles Bruce for publishing help. Linda Fuernics and Keith Whitney (via Marnie Bourbannais), Mark Jonah, Dave Hamlin, Pat Coulter, Mark Savard from Red Shred's, Donny Butler from Cap'n Holiday's, Paul Berry (and Darlene Fair) from Rock & River, Craig Whitaker from REO Rafting, and Rick Hayes from Purple Hayes for valuable river information. Don and Paula Jamieson from Squamish Kayak for promo help. Lynne Campos and Lauren Wick from the Water Survey of Canada. Trevor Marshall for mountain bike info. Monica De and John & Jean Crowe for their brutally honest critiquing and editing. Mike Crowe for his map and other help. Catrina Crowe for considering helping out as part of her holiday. Roy Williams for his computer and marketing assistance. Christian and Jocelyn Schild for their good cookin' and good lookin'. Heath Bolster for map advice. Russ Jeffrey for demanding recognition. Vic (and Rami) Tan for stopping by. Duncan Currie for his perspective. The advertisers for their faith and cash. Finally, thanks to everyone we didn't include here, but who know we should have. Sun follows rain follows sun. Paddle and flow.

Between the Covers

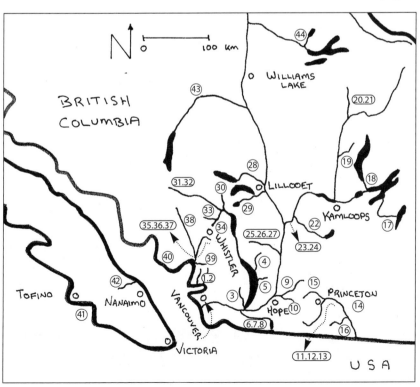

Introduction

Raging rapids, placid pools, surging seas.

In a place named after an empire and a river, one would expect some pretty outstanding whitewater. British Columbia - in particular the Southwest corner, from cosmopolitan Vancouver to the dry Thompson region, from the sunny southern Interior to snow-capped Whistler - meets and beats that expectation.

Deep canyons, broad valleys, empty beaches.

The geography and climate beg for paddlers. Richly forested mountains rise abruptly from the sea, drawing moisture and spirits up with them. In the fall and winter, the moderate temperatures of the coast's lower elevations keep this moisture liquid, permitting drysuit paddling. In the upper elevations and in the Interior, the moisture is held in reserve as snow so that the less fanatical can enjoy it in the warm spring and summer when it rushes down narrow gorges and sweeping valleys to rejoin the sea. The result is an all-year whitewater paradise.

Sparkling glaciers, cascading waterfalls, towering trees.

From this feast of delights, we have selected the most accessible rivers and ocean features - those that are easy enough to get to without the headache of expedition planning. As well, we have included rivers that will interest beginner, intermediate and advanced whitewater enthusiasts. We hope to offer experts guidance in a future book.

Soaring eagles, darting fish, lumbering bears.

While this book was written from a kayaker's perspective, canoeists and rafters may find the information useful. We have made every effort to rate the levels of difficulty based on a standard Class scale (see below).

Tight channels, plunging cataracts, vast oceans.

This book is not a guide for *how* to run a river. Our main objectives are to get you to the run, give you a sense of its difficulty, and find you a place to sleep. A significant part of the river running thrill is reading the river and responding to your interpretation. Experience is the best guide - so get out there!

Green water, blue water, whitewater!

You want it, you got it in the Southwest corner of British Columbia - Mother Nature's gift to paddlers.

3

Following is an explanation of how to use this book.
Each chapter is laid out with these headings:

CLASS

Name of River
Section (if applicable)

Directions: This gets you to the area. It does so in kilometers because we've decided to make a decision. 1 kilometer = 0.6 miles; therefore, from now on 0.6 miles will be referred to as 1 km. The road distance measurements are correct to the best of our knowledge. A few, however, may be slightly off because the tires of Jim's Land Cruiser are oversize so the odometer is skewed, and corrective arithmetic is not one of our strong points. Please forgive us for not paying more attention in school. We use the symbol ~ (which means approximately) in such cases. We indicate significant intersections with a **T** or **Y**, depending on their design.

To Take-Out:
- Sort of self-explanatory.
- If you are a seasoned local you may wish to skip the next bit, but if you are a freshie or a visitor, we hope you won't. Please keep in mind that many of the take-outs and put-ins are at Forest Service Recreation sites and other public areas. Our privilege can be denied in a snap. There are things we can do to prevent this. We should park well out of the way at take-outs and put-ins to allow for other traffic. We must not litter and we should keep nudity undemonstrative.

To Put-In:
- Ditto.
- Ditto.

Character: Here we try to give you a sense of the river's personality, whether it's playful, abusive, remote, or multi-leveled. If there is a freak hole or drop on an otherwise tame river, we try to let you know. We don't claim to have intimate knowledge of any of these rivers, just various levels of experience with them. Some we can describe in detail, others we have only enough information to write what you read. There are about six which we didn't even run for various reasons. But we at least went to each and measured distances, analyzed character and tested the frigidity of the water with cautious fingers. The rest of the information we bummed off people. (This is true for all the runs except the Chilko and Cariboo rivers. That information is completely pirated.☺)

Considerations: WHEN IN DOUBT, SCOUT. We don't hold your hand down the river by giving you a hole-by-wave-by-rapid guide. Where we think it is warranted, we will use this space to warn about dangers.

4

Season: To every river, there is a season. We guesstimate when it is. Season all depends on snowpack, rainfall, temperature, and time: all decidedly unpredictable. Where we can, we add a hydrograph that illustrates average monthly flow for each river. These show flow in cubic meters per second (cms). For the dinosaurs, the equivalent in cubic feet per second (cfs) is roughly as follows:

cms	5	10	25	50	100	150	250	500	1000	2000
cfs	200	400	900	1800	3500	5300	9000	18000	35000	71000

Class: This section describes the degree of difficulty of the river. Rivers are rated by their Class. The Class of a river can and will fluctuate with the seasons. On some rivers, more water increases a run's difficulty by adding tremendous power. On other rivers, more water decreases a run's difficulty by washing out features. A good downpour can change the Class in hours. The rating for each run in this book represents its typical Class, and does not necessarily reflect what you are experiencing when you are on it. In general, the Classes are as follows:

Class I is moving water with small waves and riffles, no obstacles.

Class II has bigger waves and rapids, but still a clear easy channel to follow.

Class III has even bigger waves with longer rapids. Some maneuvering required. Beginners and low intermediates probably want to scout from the shore. Can offer some insight into the potential power of water.

Class IV is the last of the rivers in which a person can probably get away with swimming. However, a confident roll will help ensure safety. Rapids are longer and more technical, requiring excellent maneuvering skills. Definitely a good idea to scout.

Class V rivers are multi-dimensional with very difficult features including keeper holes, powerful eddy lines, violent boils, and lengthy boulder gardens. All these rivers are scouted by teams of expert paddlers. A swim could be your last.

Class VI used to be considered unrunnable. Today, however, previous barriers are being shattered as more and more people discover video cameras. No way are these rivers recommended to anyone but the best.

- and **+** are used to differentiate levels of difficulty within classes. For example, a class III- is more difficult than a II+, but less difficult than a III.

Length of Run: We estimate the distance of the run and/or the time it takes to paddle it. These are educated guesses. We didn't use anything more technically ingenious than maps, odometers and our left brains. Oh yeah, sometimes we used a watch.

Shuttle: This is the length of drive, bike or walk required to get from the take-out to the put-in, and vice versa. If you will be kayakhitchhiking, remember you stink. Please wear your least offensive poly-pro and offer to sit in the trunk. The fewer incidents of nausea we have with kayakhitchhiker picker-uppers, the better for us all.

Camping: We have included those sites that want your cash nearest to the run, and also any that may be worth the extra drive. These sites are mostly managed by the BC Ministry of Forests (Forest Service / FS) or BC Parks (Prov. Park), but some are private.

▲ BC Ministry of Forests 1 800 689-9025 www.for.gov.bc.ca
Camping fees for Rec sites have been levied since 1999. The price depends on whether or not the site has been "enhanced" - which seems to mean someone picks up the garbage, cleans the outhouses and collects your money. You can buy a $27 pass which gets you discounts on various sites. With the pass you can stay for free or pay up to $10. The pass is valid for one year starting in the Spring. Without a pass, the prices are, of course, higher. We have listed prices when we can.

▲ BC Provincial Parks 1 800 689-9025 (Vancouver 689-9025)
www.discovercamping.ca for reservations.
Camping fees apply at all BC Park campgrounds. $12 seems to be a minimum. At some sites reservations can be made for a fee from Mar. 1 to Sept. 15. They may be made from 3 months in advance to 2 days before.

Dogs rule the world

Free Camping:
▲ There are beautiful sites in many places. They are beautiful because the people who use them keep them that way.
▲ There are ugly sites in many places. They are ugly because some of the people who use them make them that way.
▲ There are free sites everywhere if you don't mind drab surroundings and possibly being kicked off. Our experience has been that by keeping the place clean, being quiet, arriving late and leaving early we usually have no problems. How Canadian, eh?
▲ Free in BC now usually means no facilities, including outhouses. So it is up to us to shit with style: ecologically and aesthetically. For the sake of others to follow, who may well be your friends - hell, it could even be you - please dig a hole, roll a log or tip a rock; deposit; burn your paper and cover (be aware of area fire bans, contact the local Min. of Forests Fire Centre: Kamloops (250) 554-5000, Coastal (250) 951-4222, Cariboo (250) 989-2600 and, of course, be careful of fire regardless). We know we are preaching to the converted, for the most part, but for that least part - the rogue element - we must battle ignorance with information. Kayakers generally cause little damage in the forest, but we must all still do what we can to preserve these sites, because Free in BC is also becoming an endangered species. Nowhere is safe. Access is being denied and fees are being collected. The information for every site we tell you about is only good for as long as we stayed there.

Lodgings: After getting passed by a kayak-bearing BMW, we thought we should include information on how to find a warm bed and a hot shower.
✔ We have included a phone number (and email & internet addresses if available) for a local Visitor Information Center or two.
✔ For general information: 1 800 HELLO BC (435-5622) (Vancouver can drop the 1 800). Overseas (250) 387-1642. www.HelloBC.com

Food & Drink: We tell you in which town are the nearest grocery stores, restaurants and pubs.

Other Activities: If there is something else worth your while, we let you know. Included are hikes, mountain bike trails, rock-climbing areas, geographical phenomenon, and so on.

Water Gauges: We ignored these because we found all those numbers to be so much technical mumbo-jumbo. We tended to use our eyes to see if the water was low or high. We looked at the riparian zone to see whether the water was flowing amongst smooth stones (low), sharp rocks (medium), vegetation (high) or houses (flood). Some rivers on the coast, while running low, tried to fool us with vegetation levels that reached well down into the riparian zone. At first glance, then, these rivers would look like they were running high until we noticed that this vegetation (moss and lichens) was almost black, unlike the green above the actual high water mark.

Views: Although we don't generally go on about the vistas, you can be pretty sure they are rarely less than spectacular. This *is* BC. However, this being BC, almost everywhere you go you will see clearcuts - disturbing, unsightly reminders of how we get access to all these magnificent rivers. Logging roads are one of life's paradoxes: if they didn't lead to devastation, they wouldn't also lead to splendour.

Disclaimer: We have made every effort to ensure the accuracy of the information within this book. However, due to the constant nature of change, it becomes unreliable immediately after it is written. Rivers change course, roads are deactivated, property becomes private. We are not responsible for these changes nor the failure to report them before they happen. When the changes become numerous enough to warrant it, we hope to publish another edition. Your input regarding changes is greatly appreciated. Please contact us at 6594 Chukar Dr., Kamloops, BC, V2C 4T7, or scrowe69@hotmail.com.

This book is a guide to find rivers and camping sites. **It is not a guide for *how* to run rivers.** Putting yourself in a boat, then in a river, is a decision you make and one we are in no way responsible for. Respect the water and its ability to humble you. We strongly recommend that paddlers take lessons and kayak with experienced groups. We also recommend having fun.

The trick is to stay inside your boat, upside up.

Capilano River ①

Directions: The Capilano separates West and North Vancouver, which makes it only about 10 minutes from downtown. From Lions Gate Bridge, follow Marine Dr. East, or from Second Narrows Bridge, follow Hwy. 1 West, to Capilano Rd.

To Take-Out:

- ✔ Hwy. 1 bridge: on the river side of Capilano Rd., South of Hwy. 1, there is a small parking lot with a trail to the river.
- ✔ Klahanie Park: heading South on Capilano Rd., just before the lights at Marine Drive, turn Right onto hidden Curling Rd. At the STOP sign turn Right to Capilano RFC (also Evergreen Squash Club). Continue to the paved parking lot behind the baseball diamonds.

To Put-In:

- ✦ ~ 1.5 km north of Hwy. 1 on Capilano Rd., follow signs to Capilano Park Rd. on your Left. Drive to the end of the road which is a vehicle loop. Drop your boats here. You can put in below the weir (if you're thinking about it, we were told it is possible to jump the weir when the gauge is between 2.5 and 3.5, but weirs are just dangerous, period).
- ✦ For an easier put-in that misses the first rapid, walk a short way downriver from the vehicle loop to Cable Pool.

Character: A gorgeous and friendly pool-drop canyon in, if not the heart, then certainly the pancreas, of a major North American city. Run-off from the unseen, unheard streets far above cascades down the sheer walls, breeding lushness. At the Capilano Suspension Bridge crowds of suspended tourists remind you briefly of the metropolis pulsating above you. Plenty of eddy lines, headwalls and small holes, not many waves. Low water offers more play spots. High water is a flush. The water gauge is at the weir: 2 - 3.5 is low water; 3.5 - 7 is medium; 7 - 9 is high. If you can't read the gauge then don't run it.

Considerations: Watch for fallen trees. At low water, be careful of rocks in the drops.

Season: Very responsive to rain, so possible all year but best in spring and fall.

Class: Low water: III. Medium water: III+. High water: III+ to IV-. Very high water: unrunnable.

Length of Run: ~ 4.5 km to Klahanie, ~ 3.5 km to Hwy. 1.

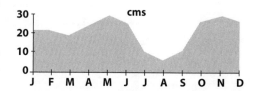

Shuttle:
~ 5 km for full run.

Camping:
Capilano RV Park
(604) 987-4722
www.capilanorvpark.com
is below the Lions Gate
bridge. It has camping
sites and RV hook-up
sites. Full facilities
include hot showers and a
laundromat. If you stay
here you can also use it as
a take-out.

Free Camping:
In Vancouver? Yeah, right.

Lodgings:
North Vancouver Visitor
Info (604) 987-4488 or
980-5332
email:
nvtour@cofcnorthvan.org
www.cofcnorthvan.org

Food & Drink: Despite
the overt sexism, we can't
help but tell you that in June 2000 the Cactus Club at Marine Drive and Pemberton had
the most stunning array of female passers-by ever recorded by our eyes. And other
places exist.

Other Activities: *Tour the fish hatchery at the put-in. *Hike Lynn Canyon Park. This is
a free alternative to the heavily commercialized Capilano Suspension Bridge. Lynn also
has a suspension bridge and some nice hikes around the canyon. Go ~ 4 km east of
Capilano or ~ 3 km west of Second Narrows Bridge on Hwy. 1. Then follow Lynn Valley
Road. Turn Right on Peters Rd. *Hike the Grouse Grind, or take the gondola, to Grouse
Mountain to drink in the sights of Vancouver (or drink within sight of Vancouver).
Continue up Capilano Rd.

Seymour River

Free spirits denied! The Seymour River in North Vancouver has become a tough one to access. The local residents, frustrated with congested residential streets, parties and vandalism, have effectively closed the area to parking. It is still possible to paddle, but you need someone to drop you off at the put-in. Also, in the summer months the primary put-in has a locked gate at the top of a long flight of stairs. You must get a key from Paddle Sports of BC, be a member of a club, and pay a deposit. At least this was true a few years ago. When we were there in June of 2000 the gate was certainly locked. Repeated phone calls to the Whitewater Kayak Association of BC for up-to-date information have gone unreturned. You try: (604) 515-6379. We are aware that all this hassle puts the Seymour a bit beyond our scope, but being that it is so close to Vancouver, we thought it should be included. More difficult sections exist upstream; however, you need permission to run these as well. Try the above number.

Directions: Cross the Second Narrows bridge from Vancouver to North Vancouver on Hwy. 1 West. The first exit on the Right puts you on Dollarton Hwy. (look for signs to Deep Cove).

To Take-Out: You will quickly cross Seymour River, then take a Right onto Riverside Drive (West). Cross the tracks and take an immediate Right onto Spicer Road. Park as close to the river as possible. (Or, more likely, arrange for your shuttle to pick you up here.)

To Put-In:
- Get back on Dollarton Hwy. (turn Right) heading east. Look for signs to Mount Seymour Park in ~ 0.5 km and turn Left onto Riverside Drive (East). Cross Mount

Seymour Parkway and continue ~ 1.2 km to Swinburne Ave. on the Left. The put-in is at the end of the lane. Resident parking only here.

✦ For the main put-in, continue ~ 0.7 km up Riverside Drive (East) to a gated path across from 2300 Chapman Way. There are 135 steps down to the water in addition to the other obstacles mentioned above. Resident parking only.

Character: Small volume. Rock gardens in low and medium water, hole gardens in high water. Continuous but easy. Good learning tool.

Considerations: Watch out for sweepers (and tow trucks if you park). You can walk out of the river almost anywhere if it is too crazy for you.

Season: All year except late summer. It is best at high water, so rainy days are good.

Class: I+ at low water. III- at high water.

Length of Run: ~ 3.5 km for the full run.

Shuttle: ~ 3.5 km.

Hey! How about keeping the nudity undemonstrative!

Camping: Capilano RV Park (604) 987-4722 www.capilanorvpark.com is below the Lions Gate bridge in West Vancouver. It has camping sites and RV hook-up sites. Full facilities include hot showers and a laundromat.

Free Camping: Ha ha ha ha ha…

Lodgings: North Vancouver Visitor Info (604) 987-4488 or 980-5332 email:nvtour@cofcnorthvan.org   www.cofcnorthvan.org

Food & Drink: Lots of everything, everywhere.

Other Activities: North Shore mountain biking. World class trails carve up the slopes above North Vancouver. Contact On Top (604) 990-9550, Deep Cove 1-800 919-2453 or John Henry's (604) 986-5534.

Chehalis River ③
(and Statlu Creek CLASS IV)

Directions: From Vancouver drive East to Mission via Hwys. 1 and 11. From there follow Hwy. 7 (Loughheed Highway) ~ 30 km until you arrive at the Sasquatch Inn . Turn Left onto Morris Valley Rd. and you will quickly come to a 4-way STOP. If you come from the Interior, from Hope drive West on Hwy. 7. Morris Valley Rd. is ~ 18 km West of Agassiz.

To Take-Out:

✦ Chehalis River bridge: from the 4-way STOP, drive straight through on Morris Valley Rd. 5.8 km to the bridge.

✦ Boulder Creek: if you want to reduce the distance of the run, you can put-in or take-out at Boulder Creek. From the 4-way STOP travel west 8.1 km on Chehalis Forest Service Rd. to a logging road that drops off to your Right. In June 2000, this road began ~ 200 m before its cut-block, but as you read this, who knows? You can confirm you have the correct road by continuing on to Boulder Creek bridge - it should

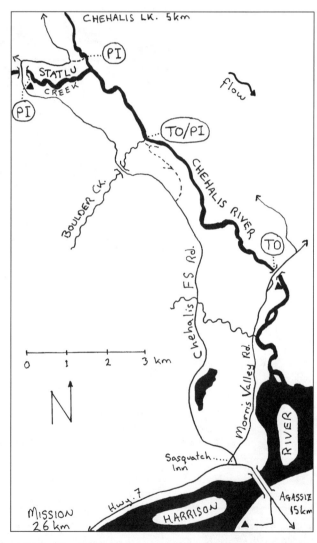

be 1.8 km further. Back at the logging road, follow it ~ 2 km, staying Right at the fork halfway. At the last bend at the bottom of the cut-block, park and walk down the little

dirt road on the Left. You can possibly drive this, but it's not far either way. When that road ends, walk down the path to the river where you come out just downstream of Boulder Creek. If you are using this as a take-out, be sure to have a look beforehand to scout a landmark.

The Chehalis Forest Service Road is an active logging road that can be closed for hauling (usually open weekends, mornings and evenings). Call Canfor (604) 796-2757 to check status. Even if closed, if you stop at the office up the road, they will probably oblige you by warning trucks coming down.

To Put-In:
- Statlu Creek: turn West at the 4-way STOP onto Chehalis FS Rd. and travel ~ 14.3 km to Statlu Creek. Put in beside the bridge.
- Chehalis River: if you want to miss Statlu and get a little more Chehalis, then continue 1.7 km past Statlu bridge and pull over and park where you see a narrow dirt road on your Right. You can judge if you want to drive this, there are lots of puddles, but there is a very small turn-around at the end. We don't recommend it. If you walk, then it will take 15 to 20 minutes altogether. At the turn-around, find a steep but good path towards the river. This deposits you at a nice drop above a pool.
- Boulder Creek: as above for Take-Out.

Character: Pool drop after pool drop on the medium-volume Chehalis. Headwalls can increase the difficulty significantly when the river is pounding. Continuous boulder garden on the Statlu.

Considerations: The river is in a canyon far removed from the road for its entire length, except for at one point (Boulder Ck.), so make sure you really want to run before you commit.

Season: Any time except late summer. The Chehalis lasts longer than Statlu. Snow can make access a problem in the winter, though. Fall rain and spring melt are best.

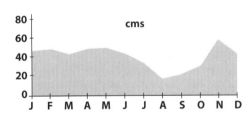

Class: Statlu IV; Chehalis III+.

Length of Run: ~ 12 km for full run. Statlu ~ 4 km, Chehalis ~ 8 km.

Shuttle: Take-out bridge → Boulder Creek: 13.9 km
→ Statlu Creek: 20.1 km
→ Chehalis put-in: 21.8 km.

14

Camping:
▲ Chehalis River Forest Service campground: on the south-east side of the take-out bridge. Medium size site. Prime riverfront sites can be used as take-outs. $10 per vehicle without a pass, $5 with. Outhouses.
▲ Chehalis Lake South FS campground: at the beginning of the river a few kilometers above the put-in. This site is good if you want to be on a lake, but it adds kilometers to your odometer. Small site. Free with FS pass. Outhouses. The access road is small and narrow, but a small RV could probably make it.
▲ Kilby Prov. Park campground: on Harrison Bay. Along Hwy. 7, drive East from Sasquatch Inn over the Harrison River bridge and take an immediate Right onto School Rd. From there follow the signs ~ 2 km. Very open, quite suburban, $12/site, outhouses.

Free Camping:
▲ There are small roads to explore above Statlu Creek where there are possible sites. The easiest, although the grubbiest, is off a small dirt road just before and to the Right of Statlu bridge. Here you can find sites beside the creek.
▲ If desperate, search for what looks like a small, old rock quarry on the West side of Morris Valley Rd., on a straight stretch about two-thirds of the way from the 4-way STOP to the bridge. Not really for tents, but it's a place to park.

Lodgings:
✔ Harrison Hot Springs Visitor Info (604) 796-3425, email: harrison@uniserve.com
www.harrison.ca
✔ Mission Visitor Info (604) 826-6914, email: email@missionchamber.bc.ca
www.missionchamber.bc.ca

Food & Drink: Groceries, pubs and restaurants in Agassiz and Mission. If you just want to put something in your stomach, the Sasquatch Inn is near the 4-way STOP. A convenience store is down the road to the east.

Other Activities: *Hike the canyon. Begin at the Forest Service day use site across the take-out bridge on the Left. Walk through the old campsites (which may again be in use; in June 2000 there were some land claim issues that caused the FS to close them) and find the very well worn path(s) that follow the north rim of the canyon. We didn't hike the whole way so we can't tell you how far it goes, but it gives you great vantage points to get a sense of the river's character. *Rock climbing is also available on this trail. It doesn't looked well-used, so bring a brush, but someone has put bolts on a 8 m wall. Some lines are still clear for your own pro, too. *Right beside Morris Valley Rd. about halfway between the 4-way STOP and the bridge is another small bolted area. The entire region is made up of cliffs. For the adventurous, climbing can be found in many places.

Big Silver Creek   ④

Directions: From Vancouver, drive East on Hwy. 1 or 7 to Agassiz. From Hope, drive West on Hwy. 1 or 7 to Agassiz. From Agassiz follow Hwy. 9 north to Harrison Hot Springs. At the **T** at the end of the road (at the south shore of the lake), turn Right and head out of town. Follow signs towards Sasquatch Park. At the one STOP sign, turn Right. At the intersection with the road to Deer and Hicks lakes, stay Left on the gravel Harrison East Forest Road. Eventually cross Cogburn Creek and turn Left. Continue to Silver River.

To Take-Out: Look for the take-out at Silver River on Harrison Lake. Check that you can take-out on the south side of the log yard.

To Put-In: Continue through the log yard, past Hornet Creek bridge, and ~ 2 km further to Clear Creek Rd. Park out of the way in the sand pit beside the intersection. The overgrown, unmarked trail begins just to the North of, and across from, the Clear Creek Rd. junction. Have a good look on foot - you won't find it from your car. The trail is very steep and challenging when you are carrying an armful of heavy plastic. The put-in is below a beautiful, but challenging, drop.

Character: A gentle learning tool. Medium volume. There are waves at Hornet Creek junction. The creek (at this point really a river) mellows out to flat water as you near the lake.

Considerations: Watch for sweepers and log jams. Getting to the put-in is the greatest challenge.

Season: Spring and summer. May to August.

Class: II-.

Length of Run: ~ 7 km; 1.5 hours.

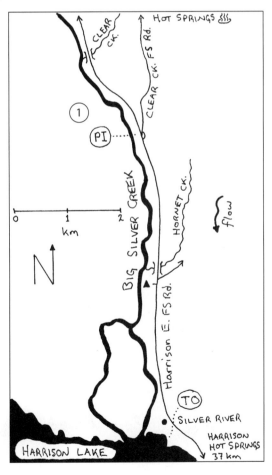

16

Shuttle: ~ 5 km.

Camping: See the Cogburn Creek section for nearby sites.

Free Camping:
▲ Hornet Creek. ~ 200 m South of Hornet Creek bridge is a gravel and sand bar beside the river. A wave train sits in front. You can drive down to the site, or park beside the road and walk the very short distance.
▲ See the Cogburn Creek section for nearby sites.

Lodgings: Harrison Hot Springs Visitor Info (604) 796-3425
email: harrison@uniserve.com   www.harrison.ca

Food & Drink: Harrison Hot Springs has grocery stores, restaurants and pubs.

Other Activities: *Soak in Clear Creek Hot Springs. Drive as far as you can up Clear Creek Rd., then start hiking. We didn't do the dip, but we were told it can take a couple of hours to get there. A hot tub has been installed by locals, but the springs are free. *If you go to Harrison Hot Springs Resort, the only thing that has to walk is your money.

Other: Carry a spare and a jack. Harrison East is notorious for puncturing tires.

Just another lousy tributary to be awed by

Cogburn Creek ⑤

Directions: From Vancouver, drive East on Hwy. 1 or 7 to Agassiz. From Hope, drive West on Hwy. 1 or 7 to Agassiz. From Agassiz follow Hwy. 9 north to Harrison Hot Springs. At the **T** at the end of the road (at the south shore of the lake), turn Right and head out of town. Follow signs towards Sasquatch Park. At the one STOP sign, turn Right. At the intersection with the road to Deer and Hicks lakes, stay Left on the gravel Harrison East Forest Road. Continue ~ 20 km to Cogburn Creek.

To Take-Out:

➤ Before you reach the logging yard, look for a take-out along the lakeshore.

➤ For a shorter run that misses only a short stretch of rapids and a lot of flat water paddling, continue along the road. Turn Left at the intersection past the log yard and drive to the bridge over Cogburn Creek.

To Put-In:

➤ Over the bridge, turn Right and drive a little more than a kilometer until you find a pullout on the Right. The creek is a short, steep scramble away.

➤ You can reach the same put-in, but across the creek, by driving up the other side (southeast side) of the creek from the bridge. At the intersection that will take you back to the first take-out, turn Left and cross Talc Creek. Shortly after, there is a dirt road on the Left. The end of this is the put-in.

Character: Short, quick, pushy, continuous boulder or hole garden. Small volume.

Considerations: Watch for fallen trees.

Season: Spring. April to June, possibly early July.

Class: III+ to IV at high water.

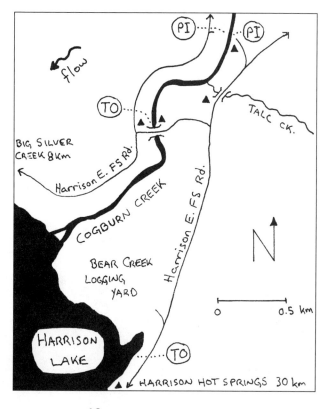

18

Length of Run: ~ 3km for full run. ~ 1 km for the short run.

Shuttle: ~ 3.5 km for full run. ~ 1km if you take-out at the bridge.

Camping:
▲ Cogburn Creek FS campground. Open sites between the road and the lake. Pretty but abused. Expect company on weekends. Outhouse. Free with $27 pass or $8/site.
▲ Bear Creek FS campground. Shady but open. Beside the lake a few kilometers south of Cogburn. Small. Outhouse. Free with $27 pass or $8/site.
▲ BC Parks campgrounds at Hicks and Deer lakes in Sasquatch Park. $12/site.

Free Camping:
▲ On either side of the take-out bridge over Cogburn.
▲ Beside Talc Creek, just to the Left before you cross the bridge over Talc.
▲ At the 2nd put-in.

Lodgings: Harrison Hot Springs Visitor Info (604) 796-3425
email: harrison@uniserve.com   www.harrison.ca

Food & Drink: Groceries, restaurants and pubs in Harrison Hot Springs.

Other Activities: Soak in Clear Creek Hot Springs. See Big Silver Creek for directions.

Other: Carry a spare and a jack. Harrison East is notorious for puncturing tires. Interestingly, in another one of the coincidences that help make life entertaining, as I wrote the last sentence we passed by a garage in Mission where they were repairing the tire of a van we saw at Cogburn Creek. You can also get repaired in Agassiz.

Chilliwack River
In General

The Chilliwack river has something for everyone. It is a long river with a variety of classes of whitewater, many access points, and a long season. It is possible to make up your own run of whatever distance you choose. We have divided the river into three runs that are distinct from one another in terms of level of difficulty. This section covers general information about Pointa Vista to Vedder Crossing, Slesse Creek to Pointa Vista, and the Canyon. Following are sections which explain each run specifically.

Directions: From Vancouver, follow Hwy. 1 East to Sardis (Chilliwack). From points east, follow Hwy. 1 West to Sardis, then take Vedder Rd. and follow signs to Cultus Lake. You will pass through the town of Sardis and eventually come to the Chilliwack River at Vedder Crossing. Across the bridge, at the restaurant, is the take-out for Pointa Vista to Vedder; otherwise, do not cross the bridge, but rather turn Left onto Chilliwack Lake Rd.

Considerations: This river is very popular with fishers, so please be courteous and avoid confrontations whenever possible. Also be careful of tangled and discarded fishing lines hanging from trees.

Camping: There are a number of Forest Service Rec sites all along the river, many of which also serve as take-outs and put-ins. These include:
▲ Chipmunk. Large, outhouses, $27 pass + $5 or $10/night.
▲ Thurston Meadows. Moderate, outhouses, pass + $5 or $10/night.
▲ Tamihi. Moderate, outhouses, pass + $5 or $10/night. Cross the Tamihi bridge, then take an immediate Right and cross Tamihi Ck.
▲ Tamihi Rapids. Small, outhouse, pass or $8/night. Cross the Tamihi bridge and park on the Left. This was a heavily abused spot until restoration began in 2000.
▲ Allison Pool. Small, outhouse, pass or $8/night.
▲ Rapids. Small, outhouse, pass or $8/night. This site is on the north side of the river.
▲ Camp Foley. Small, outhouse, pass or $8/night.
▲ Riverside. Moderate, outhouse, pass or $8/night.
▲ Chilliwack Lake Provincial Park campground. Large, full facilities except showers. $12/night. ~ 14 km past Camp Foley.
▲ Cultus Lake Prov. Park campground. Very large, full facilities, reservations accepted. Cross Vedder, then follow Cultus Lake Rd., then Columbia Valley Hwy. for 16 km.

Free Camping: The north side of the river, on Chilliwack Bench FS Rd. west of Camp Foley, has some free camping still available, but it is disappearing quickly. You will have to search for what is left.

Lodgings: Chilliwack Visitor Info (604) 858-8121, 1 800 567-9535
www.tourismchilliwack.com

Food & Drink: Groceries, restaurants and pubs are in Sardis and Chilliwack. The restaurant at Vedder Crossing has long been a paddlers' hangout.

Other Activities: *Marked motocross trails are on the north side of the river. Cross the bridge at the Camp Foley put-in for the Canyon and you will soon see (or hear) them on the Chilliwack Bench FS Road. *There are many hikes in the area. A short one to Lindeman Lake begins before Chilliwack Lake at Post Creek Rec site on Chilliwack Lake Road. *Spelunk Chipmunk Caves. ~ 1 km downstream from Foley is a dirt road that leads to the river. This is a possible put-in for the Canyon as well. From here, walk downriver to a point across the Chilliwack from where Chipmunk Creek flows in. Bring flashlights to explore the two caves. Helmets are a good idea too. You can also paddle to here.

Early evening glare below Tamihi bridge

Chilliwack River

Pointa Vista to Vedder

Chilliwack Lake Road follows the river, and therefore there are a number of places to put-in and take-out. Included here are the most popular.

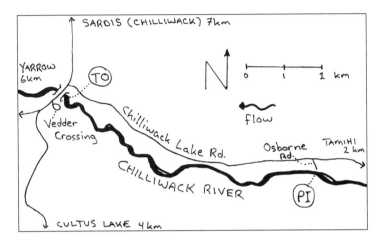

To Take-Out: The take-out is at the restaurant parking lot at Vedder Crossing.

To Put-In: Follow Chilliwack Lake Rd. ~ 7 km to Osborne Road on the Right, which is just past Pointa Vista café. Drive to the end of Osborne and park on the side. Be aware of the property owner's rights at the end of the road as he has made efforts to keep kayakers off his land.

Character: Braided, medium volume. A good place to practice eddy lines and feel mildly turbulent water. Putting in from the riprap at the end of Osborne Rd. may very well be the most difficult feature of the run.

Considerations: Be careful of sweepers and logjams. This section of river is always changing, so be prepared to scout. Be careful of tangled and discarded fishing lines hanging from trees.

Season: Spring and fall. Summer flood is a washout. Too braided for winter.

Class: II.

Length of Run: ~ 7.5 km.

Shuttle: ~ 7 km.

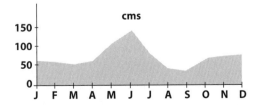

22

Chilliwack River

Slesse to Pointa Vista

The following take-outs can also be used as put-ins, depending on how far you want to paddle.

To Take-Out:

- ✦ Pointa Vista. From Vedder, follow Chilliwack Lake Rd. ~ 7 km to Osborne Road on the Right, which is just past Pointa Vista café. Drive to the end of Osborne and park on the side. Be aware of the property owner's rights at the end of the road as he has made efforts to keep kayakers off his land.
- ✦ Dirty campsite. Continue along Chilliwack Lake Rd. ~ 3 km. ~ 300 m before Tamihi bridge, you will find what was a filthy campsite in 2000 on your Right.
- ✦ Below Tamihi Rapid. Cross the bridge and park on the Left.
- ✦ Above Tamihi Rapid. Drive ~ 0.5 km further, above the rapid, and look for a path to the river on the Left.
- ✦ Allison Pool. Continue ~ 3 km to this Forest Service Rec site. At high water the river runs adjacent, but at low water you must walk across an island to the river. Good park 'n' play spot just up river along the road.
- ✦ Thurston Meadows. ~ 3 km further is this FS site.

To Put-In:

- ✦ Use any of the above take-outs, or:
- ✦ Below Slesse Creek. Drive ~ 2.5 km past Thurston to just before the bridge over Slesse. You will find parking on the Left.
- ✦ Slesse Creek. Put into Slesse Creek at the bridge.

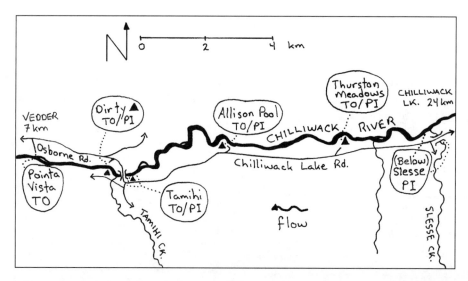

Character: Varied features, almost continuous. Medium volume. Anything big is a pool-drop except for Tamihi, which is a boulder garden and easily visible from the bridge that crosses it. Wave trains, canyon eddies and boulder gardens.

Considerations: Watch for sweepers and fishers.

Season: All year. Spring runoff offers the biggest ride.

Class: III to III+. One IV (Tamihi).

Length of Run: ~ 13 km for full run.

Shuttle: ~ 12 km for full run.

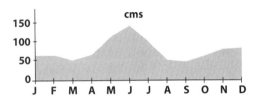

Tamihi rapid taken with a nervous hand.

Chilliwack River ⑧
The Canyon

To Take-Out: From Vedder, drive ~ 21.2 km along Chilliwack Lake Rd. until you reach a bridge over Slesse Creek. Park before the bridge on the Left.

To Put-In: Continue upstream for ~ 7 km to a bridge over the Chilliwack. Cross the bridge and then take the first Left into Camp Foley FS Rec site.

Character: Fast, pushy, continuous whitewater with occasional drops. The few eddies available are small. For this reason, for your first time, we recommend that you paddle with someone who knows the run. At high water this is a relentless run. In low water there are bony boulder gardens and pool-drops.

Considerations: Watch for fallen logs and boulders in drops at low water. For your first time, use beer (or whatever you have) to bribe a veteran to lead you.

Season: All year if you're up for it. July and August are best for water level and temperature. The river will rise quickly with rainfall. The volume of water is generally about $1/2$ of what is recorded at Vedder.

Class: IV.

Length of Run: ~ 7.5 km. 2 hours with little play.

Shuttle: ~ 7 km.

Not so pretty in high water

Finding a hole in early autumn

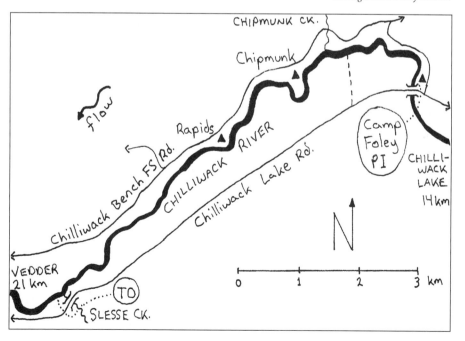

Coquihalla River (9)

Directions: From Vancouver follow Hwy. 1 East to Hope. From the Fraser Canyon, follow Hwy. 1 West to Hope. From Hope, follow Hwy. 5 North (Coquihalla Hwy.) ~ 7 km to the first bridge over the river. From the Interior, follow Hwy. 5 South to ~ 7 km before Hope. From the southern Interior, follow Hwy. 3 West to the interchange with Hwy. 5. Here turn north and drive ~ 3 km to the first bridge over the river. **This is the Kawkawa interchange.** There are roads on both sides of the river for the most part. South of the Kawkawa interchange, where Hwy. 5 crosses the Coquihalla, Hwy. 5 runs along the East shore and Othello Rd. on the West. North of Kawkawa, Hwy. 5 runs along the West shore, and North of Lear bridge the old Coquihalla (Pipeline) road is on the East. Because of this there are many possible put-ins and take-outs. Here are some, as from Kawkawa interchange:

To Take-Out:
- Othello Tunnels. Follow signs ~ 4 km west of Kawkawa interchange on Othello Rd. From the parking lot walk towards the tunnels to look for a good take-out spot. **Do not** miss this take-out because below is the Coquihalla Canyon ☠ .
- Othello Tunnels campground. ~ 3km west of Kawkawa on Othello Rd. Across and just upstream from here is a small pullout beside the river. Eddies are small and tight.
- Kawkawa interchange. Where you like.
- Lear bridge. At Kawkawa, find the dirt road that runs North, parallel to Hwy. 5. It begins at the exit/entrance ramp on the East side of the highway (West side of the river). This is Pipeline. Drive ~ 2.5 km North to Lear.

To Put-In:
- Sowaqua Creek. ~ 12 km North of Kawkawa on Hwy. 5. Cross the bridge and exit the highway. Drive to the downstream side of the bridge. This is only accessible to north-bound traffic. To return south from here, follow Pipeline Rd. or continue north on Hwy. 5 ~3 km to Carolin Mines U-turn route.
- Lear. See the 4th take-out.
- Kawkawa interchange.

Character: Multiple and varied features. Something for everyone. Many of the sections are visible from the highway, although more are visible from a tall vehicle due to the guard rails. Continuous boulder gardens from Sowaqua gradually transform into pool-drops. A wide river, so low water is very bony. Medium water has boofs galore, waves and eddy lines. High water makes for some big holes and fast water.

Considerations: No constrictions, so log jams should not be a factor. Do not miss the last take-out before the Canyon ☠ .

27

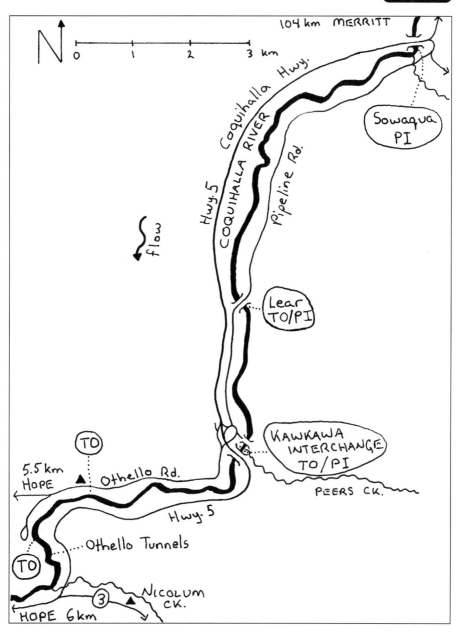

Season: Possible all winter if it rains, but best with run-off: April - July.

Class: III+ to IV at high water.

Length of Run: ~ 16 km for full run.

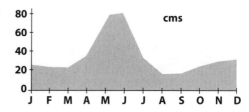

Shuttle: Sowaqua   ➡   Lear: 14.5 km
                       ➡   Kawkawa: 12 km
                       ➡   Othello Tunnels campground: 15 km
                       ➡   Othello: 16 km

Camping:
▲ Othello Tunnels campground is ~ 3 km from Kawkawa on Othello Rd.
▲ The Nicolum Provincial Park campground is a medium-sized site. Outhouses, firewood and fresh water tap. ~ 3 km south of Kawkawa on Hwy. 5, turn onto Hwy. 3 and drive ~ 2 km.
▲ Coquihalla Campground is at the end of Othello Rd. where it crosses the Coquihalla at the east end of Hope. This site is ~ 5.5 km west of Othello Tunnels campground.

Free Camping: There are numerous sites beside the river. You can access them from the highway or from Pipeline Rd.

Lodgings: Hope Visitor Info (604) 869-2021, email: hopechmb@uniserve.com www.hopechamber.bc.ca

Food & Drink: Groceries, restaurants and pubs are in Hope.

Other Activities: Stroll the Coquihalla Canyon through the Othello Tunnels. Have a look at why you want to take-out before you float into here. The series of old railway tunnels now make for a unique walk.

The highway has transformed the river bank in some places with riprap

Nicolum Creek ⑩

Directions: From Vancouver, follow Hwy. 1 East to Hope. From Hope, follow Hwy. 5 North (and from Kamloops, on Hwy. 5 South, turn before Hope) then follow Hwy. 3 (Crowsnest {Hope - Princeton} Hwy.) towards Princeton. Just 2 km along, turn Left into Nicolum Provincial Park. From Princeton, find the Park just before Hwy. 3 joins Hwy. 5 (Coquihalla). The entire run can be scouted from the highway.

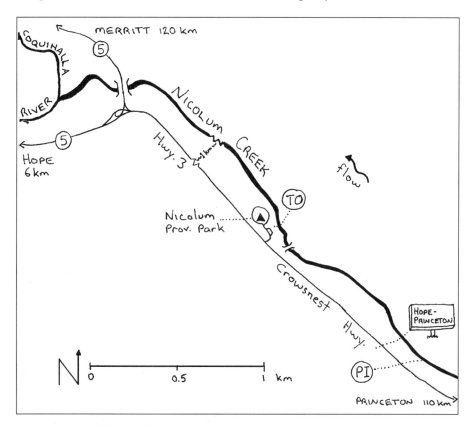

To Take-Out: You can park in the day-use area, or if you are camping, try to get site #1. This site offers a good take-out below the most difficult drop. Even if someone is already there, they may allow you to walk through their site.

To Put-In: Back on Hwy. 3, drive East ~ 1 km. There is no pull-out, so you may want to drop off your gear and leave the vehicle at the take-out. It is a short walk back to the put-in. If you do want to park your vehicle, drive ~ 200 m past the wooden HOPE-PRINCETON highway sign and pull well off the road. You really can put-in anywhere you like, as the highway follows the creek.

Character: Short, small, narrow, quick. Continuous boulder gardens and drops.

Considerations: Watch for fallen logs.

Season: Short. Spring run-off. Best in June, possible May to early July.

Class: IV.

Length of Run: ~ 1 km.

Shuttle: ~ 1km.

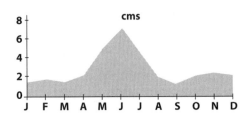

Camping: The Nicolum Provincial Park campground is a medium-sized site. Outhouses, firewood and fresh water tap.

Free Camping: See Coquihalla River section for information on nearby free camping.

Lodgings: Hope Visitor Info (604) 869-2021, email: hopechmb@uniserve.com www.hopechamber.bc.ca

Food & Drink: Groceries, restaurants and pubs are in Hope.

Other Activities: View the Hope Slide. See where a mountainside fell on unsuspecting motorists in 1965. Continue east on Hwy. 3 a few kilometers and look for signs.

Just above campsite #1

Commotion of motion

Similkameen River
In General

This section covers general information about Above the Falls, Below the Falls, and the Canyon. The following sections explain each run specifically.

Directions: From Vancouver, travel to Hope on Hwy. 1, then follow Hwy. 3 (Crowsnest {Hope-Princeton} Hwy.) towards Princeton. Pass through Manning Park until you are at Eastgate (the park's eastern boundary), ~ 230 km from Vancouver. This puts you near Above the Falls. From points east follow Hwy. 3 West to Princeton. From the north take Hwy. 5A South from Merritt. Driving to Princeton gets you to the take-out of the Canyon. See the appropriate sections for further details.

Camping:
▲ Manning Provincial Park has numerous sites, the nicest of which requires reservations and more money (Lightning Lake). The closest is Mule Deer.
▲ Copper Creek FS campground. At Copper Creek (Placer - Similkameen FS Rd.) bridge. Free with $27 pass, $10 without. Small. Outhouse.

Free Camping:
▲ Above the Falls put-in. There is an open meadow with trees and riverfront sites. See directions to the put-in.
▲ Beside the river off Pasayten FS Rd. This is just east of Eastgate along a straight stretch of Hwy. 3. Turn off to the Right, but don't go over the bridge; instead follow a parallel road on the Right that slopes down to the river.
▲ The old Placer - Similkameen FS Rd. take-out for Below the Falls. Large, open area with numerous clean riverfront sites. See directions to the take-out.
▲ Copper Creek bridge. Everywhere the FS isn't, is free.

Lodgings:
✔ Manning Park Resort (250) 840-8822, email: info@manningparkresort.com
   www.manningparkresort.com
✔ Princeton Visitor Info (250) 295-3103, email: chamber@nethop.net
   www.town.princeton.bc.ca

Food & Drink: Princeton has grocery stores, pubs and restaurants.

Other Activities: Hike part of the Canyon. From the East shore of Copper Creek bridge you can walk (or drive partway on rough road) downstream and scout the top of the Canyon.

Similkameen River ⑪

Above the Falls

Hwy. 3 runs along the river, so scouting is easy. That also means there are plenty of places to get in and out of your boat. The following are obvious spots:

To Take-Out: From Eastgate, on Hwy. 3, drive downstream 4.8 km to a large pull-off on the Right, just before the road begins climbing into a canyon. This is the take-out.

Directly downstream from this take-out is continuous Class 2 that ends in Similkameen Falls ☠. It is possible to take-out above the falls, but we don't recommend it.

To Put-In: From the take-out drive back towards Eastgate 1.4 km until you see a clearing on the Left with two turn-offs to it.

Character: A great tool for learning and practicing. Mostly small volume (although Pasayten River flows in near the end to double the volume), slow moving, nothing scary to grab and keep you. Short. High water will wash it out. Ass-bitin' cold early in the season; swimming not recommended.

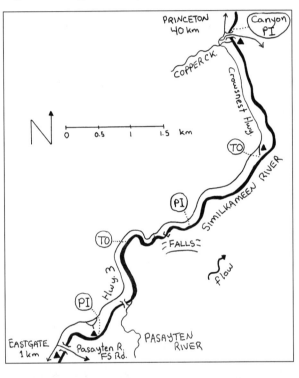

Considerations: Scout from the highway.

Season: May to July.

Class: II to II+.

Length of Run: ~ 1.5 km.

Shuttle: 1.4 km. Nice walk beside the river.

33

Similkameen River (12)
Below the Falls

We have reversed To Take-Out and To Put-In because it is easier to explain. See Above the Falls for a map.

To Put-In: Coming from Vancouver, pass Similkameen Falls on your right and follow the road as it curves to the left. Immediately on your Right is a medium sized pull-out. Pull out. From Princeton, it is best to drive past the falls, turn around, then use the above directions. Walk back to the point of the corner and scramble down the steep, loose bank. Watch out for broken glass and other debris of the wicked and the weak. Just to the Left of the point is an eddy.

To Take-Out: ~ 1.8 km downstream from the put-in is the old Placer - Similkameen Forest Service Rd. (deactivated) on the Right. Keep your eyes open as it is just around a left-hand corner and the sign is set back in the trees. No problem if you miss it, you can turn around 50 m down the road.

Character: Bone-numbing cold in June. Straight-forward. No surprises. Short. Quick.

Considerations: Most of the run can be scouted from the highway. Look for pull-outs.

Season: May to July.

Class: III.

Length of Run: ~ 1.8 km.

Shuttle: ~ 1.8 km.

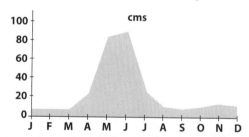

Camping at the take-out

Similkameen River ⑬
The Canyon

To Take-Out: In Princeton, Hwy. 3 crosses the Similkameen at the Blue bridge. You can't miss it, it's blue. Park on the south-east side.

To Put-In: From Princeton, follow Hwy. 3 West towards Manning Park for ~ 40 km. The put-in is at Copper Creek. Look for the sign for Placer Mountain (or Creek) Forest Service Road, on your Left, where the high-way takes a descending, tight left bend to cross Copper Creek. This is ~ 20 km east of Eastgate. Drive ~ 200 m to the bridge.

Character: Low and medium water offer exciting pool-drops and flat water. If you walk downriver from the put-in on the south side of the river you will soon come to the first

drop. If you feel comfortable running this drop, then you are laughing the rest of the way. The run begins with some Class III - IV drops, then continues with a long stretch of flat water, interspersed with the odd drop. We suggest paddling with a large group so that you have plenty of conversation to pass the time. At the end of the canyon itself is another series of III - IV drops. Here the canyon pinches in for the last time. The section is recognizable by a conveyor bridge that is suspended about 200 m above the beginning of the rapid, and its end is signalled by an overhead pipeline bridge. Afterwards it is a long paddle of Class II drops that eventually mellows out to flatness. There are some good surf waves in the drops. High water pushes through the canyon quickly, washing out some features, but making others more difficult; indeed, much more difficult.

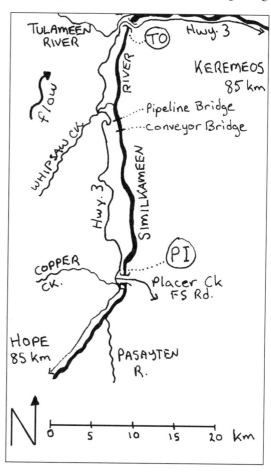

Considerations: Watch for fallen trees in narrow chutes. Everything can be scouted from shore if in doubt.

Season: Definitely best in July, when the chaos of melting snow is subsiding. Usually bony by August.

Class: IV. High water: V-

Length of Run: ~ 40 km. Because of the length of the run, we don't recommend you use it as your season opener. The canyon section can take 3 - 4 hours. The bottom, 2 - 3 hours.

Shuttle: ~ 40 km. Kayakhitch-hiking is not recommended.

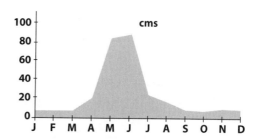

Similkameen River (14)
Bromley to Stemwinder

Directions: From Vancouver, follow Hwy. 1 East to Hope. From there, follow Hwy. 5 then Hwy. 3 East to Princeton. From the north, take Hwy. 5A South from Merritt to Princeton. From the east, follow Hwy. 3 West to Hedley (this is near the take-out).

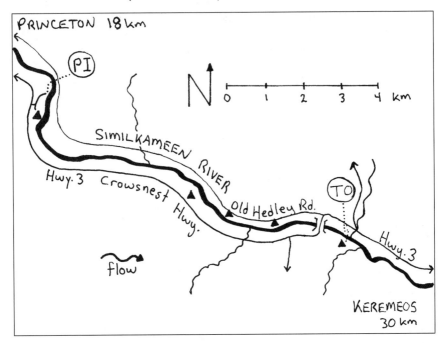

To Take-Out: From Princeton, drive along Hwy. 3 East ~ 30 km to a bridge over the Similkameen. From this bridge, continue ~ 1.5 km to Stemwinder Provincial Park on your Right.

To Put-In: Drive back towards Princeton on Hwy. 3 West ~ 11km to Bromley Rock Provincial Park on the Right. Park in the day-use area.

Character: Medium to large volume, easy, waves, great learning tool.

Considerations: Only one rapid of any significance (III) about 2/3 of the way down. Portageable.

Season: Mid-April to mid-July.

Class: II to III at high levels.

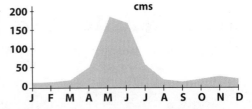

37

Length of Run: ~ 11.5 km.

Shuttle: ~ 11 km.

Camping:
▲ Bromley Rock BC Park at the put-in.
▲ Stemwinder BC Park at the take-out.
▲ There are a number of FS sites along the north shore of the river. When at the bridge over the Similkameen, instead of driving east towards the take-out, turn west and follow Old Hedley Rd.
▲ Kendicks's RV Park is ~ 5km east of Bromley on Hwy. 3. Hot showers.

Free Camping:
▲ On the north shore of the river there may be sites still available. Unless there is a sign saying 'No Camping', try it.
▲ If you don't mind a bit of a drive, see the section titled Similkameen River: In General.

Lodgings:
✔ Princeton Visitor Info (250) 295-3103, email: chamber@nethop.net www.town.princeton.bc.ca
✔ Hedley Visitor Info (250) 292-8422.

Food & Drink: Princeton has grocery stores, pubs and restaurants.

Other Activities: Before the bridge there is a good boulder to slide down or drop off.

Sliding down and dropping off, with faith in gravity

Tulameen River

Low water as seen from Hwy. 3

Directions: From Vancouver, follow Hwy. 1 East to Hope. From there, follow Hwy. 3 East to Princeton. Alternatively, from Hope you can follow Hwy. 5 North (Coquihalla) past the toll booth. Exit on the first right after the toll booth. It is best to obtain an FS Recreation map or a Backroads Mapbook for this route as it involves a few intersections. From the north, take Hwy. 5A South from Merritt to Princeton. From the east, follow Hwy. 3 West to Princeton.

To Take-Out: From Princeton, follow signs leading to Coalmont and Tulameen. At the north end of town you will cross the Brown Bridge.

To Put-In:
- After the Brown Bridge, turn Left and follow Tulameen Rd. ~ 20 km to the turnoff to Coalmont. Drive down to the bridge over the Tulameen.
- For the Granite Creek put-in, continue ~ 1km past the bridge on Granite Creek Rd. Turn Left at the intersection, cross the bridge over Granite Ck. and turn Left into the campground.

Character: Medium volume. Varied with slow, broad braided sections, a boulder garden, one tough drop, and flat water at the end.

Considerations: Tulameanie Drop is the freak on this otherwise tame river. After the boulder garden about halfway down, look on the Left for a railroad tunnel. Scout from the left bank. This is a IV to V- drop depending on water level. Portageable.

Season: Mid-April to mid-July. With enough rain it is possible at other times of the year.

Class: II with a III- boulder garden and a IV to V- drop.

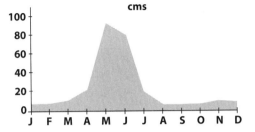

Length of Run: ~ 21 km for full run.

Shuttle: ~ 20 km.

Camping:
▲ Granite Creek FS site at the 2nd put-in.
▲ Otter Lake B.C. Park is 32 km from Princeton on the Tulameen Rd. past Coalmont.

Free Camping:
▲ If you find a site without a 'No Camping' sign, try it.
▲ Please see the sections on Similkameen River: In General and Bromley to Stemwinder.

Lodgings: Princeton Visitor Info (250) 295-3103, email: chamber@nethop.net www.town.princeton.bc.ca

Food & Drink: Princeton has grocery stores, pubs and restaurants.

Other Activities: Explore old ghost towns in this area with a rich mining history. Contact the Visitor Info (see Lodgings).

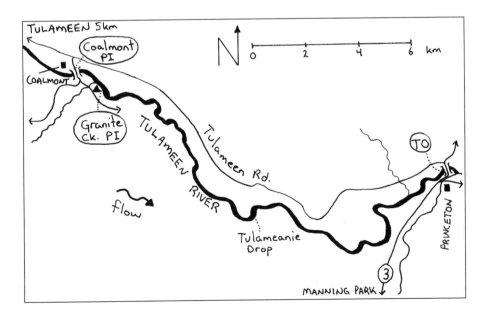

Ashnola River (16)

The Ashnola has a variety of stretches to paddle, ranging from Class II in low water to possibly V in high water. When we discovered it in mid-July, the water level was quite low; therefore, we didn't paddle every section. We could discern, however, that this is a very energetic, entertaining river - an impression confirmed by the section we did run. The road follows the entire river, so it is easy to pick your own route. We have included details on the section we paddled.

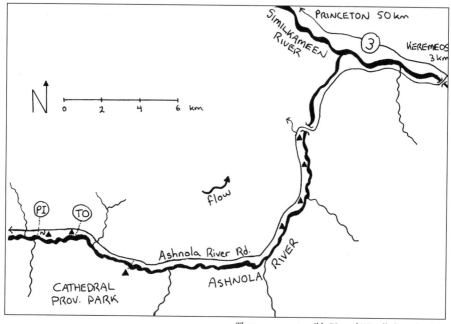

There are many possible PIs and TOs all along the river

Directions: From Vancouver, follow Hwy. 1 East to Hope, then Hwy. 3 East through Princeton. When ~ 3 km West of Keremeos, follow the signs to Cathedral Provincial Park. You will cross the Similkameen River onto the Ashnola River Rd. From points north and east, drive to Keremeos on Hwys. 3A and 3, respectively. Pass through Keremeos and look for the Cathedral Park signs ~ 3 km west of town. ~ 10 km from Hwy. 3, Ashnola River Rd. becomes gravel. At this point, kilometer markers begin reading at 0.

To Take-Out: Just before the 18 km marker, there is a small campsite beside the river.

To Put-In: Continue along the road for ~ 2.3 km until you see a small dirt road on the Left, just after the 20 km marker. This road takes a couple of tight bends then stops. Park here and walk down to the river on the Right.

Character: Continuous whitewater: boulder gardens and some pool-drops. Small volume, shallow. Like a mini Bridge River.

Considerations: Watch for sweepers and logs - we encountered three.

Season: May to early July.

Class: Low water - non-pushy III to IV with a couple of IV+ drops. High water - possibly V drops.

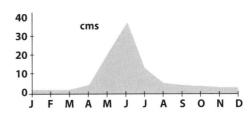

Length of Run: ~ 2.3 km. 1 hour.

Shuttle: ~ 2.3 km.

Camping:
▲ BC Parks has campgrounds along the river. Outhouses.
▲ BC Min. of Forests has campgrounds along the river. Outhouses.

Free Camping:
▲ At the take-out.
▲ At the put-in.
▲ There are a number of free sites all along the river.

Lodgings:
✔ Osoyoos Visitor Info (250) 495-7142, 1 888 676-9667,
   email: tourism@osoyooschamber.bc.ca
✔ Penticton Visitor Info (250) 493-4055, 1 800 663-5052
✔ Princeton Visitor Info (250) 295-3103,
   email: chamber@nethop.net   www.town.princeton.bc.ca

Food & Drink: Groceries, restaurants and pubs are in Keremeos, Osoyoos, Penticton and Princeton.

Other Activities: Hike in the beautiful, lake-pocked mountains of Cathedral Provincial Park (250) 494-6500.

One of the trickier drops

Shuswap River ⑰

Directions: From Kamloops, follow Hwy. 1 East to Monte Creek, then Hwy. 97 South to Vernon, then Hwy. 97A North ~ 36 km to Enderby. From Kelowna, follow Hwy. 97 North to Vernon, then Hwy. 97A North to Enderby. From points east, follow Hwy. 1 West to Sicamous, then Hwy. 97A South to Enderby.

To Take-Out: When in Enderby, turn East onto Enderby - Mabel Lake Rd. in the center of town. Drive ~ 28.5 km to a small dirt road on the Right just before the main road bends left and rises up a small hill. This is a private road but you can park a couple of cars off to the side and another across Mabel Lake Rd. When

Warming up and goofing off

you are on the river, look for this take-out immediately after the last ledge drop on river Right, past the Elbow.

To Put-In:
- For the Kingfisher put-in, continue towards Mabel Lake ~ 2 km until you reach the bridge over Kingfisher Creek. A short dirt road leading to the river is just before this bridge. There is a sign saying no camping or overnight parking.
- If you want a flat water warm-up, then continue ~ 0.5 km past the bridge, then follow the sign to the Right that says Public Access to Lake. This takes you to a marina where you can read the water gauge.

Character: Large volume, short. The entire run can be scouted from shore following fisher's paths on the north bank. The character changes with the water level. At high water it is a fast wash with few features. Medium volume offers multi-directional water that keeps you guessing. Low water entertains with plenty of play spots around the ledges.

Considerations: Watch for logs and other debris, especially at runoff. Big Eddy can attract plenty of wood.

Season: Possible year-round, but the biggest water is in June. July is probably best.

Class: III to IV depending on water level. Beyond the take-out to Cooke Ck. FS site is II-.

Length of Run: < 3 km.

Shuttle: ~ 2 km.

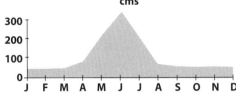

Camping:
▲ Kingfisher campground and RV park is between the take-out and Kingfisher put-in.
▲ Cooke Creek FS campground, beside the Shuswap, is ~ 5.5 km downstream from the take-out. Outhouses.
▲ There are a number of FS Rec sites up Cooke Grassy FS Rd. north of Cooke Ck. FS site, including Dale Lake ~ 7 km.

Free Camping: Most property around the river is private, so be very careful if you choose your own site.

Lodgings: Enderby Visitor Info (250) 838-6727, email: echamber@jetstream.net www.enderby.com/chamber

Food & Drink: Groceries, restaurants and pubs are in Enderby and Vernon.

Other Activities: Hike the Enderby Cliffs. From Enderby drive ~ 2 km east on Mabel Lake Rd. Turn left onto Brash Allen Rd. When the road turns to the right you will see a gap in the white fence. This is the trailhead. Permission is required as the trail passes through private land. Contact Hans Walter Hirth (250) 838-9755. Foot traffic only.

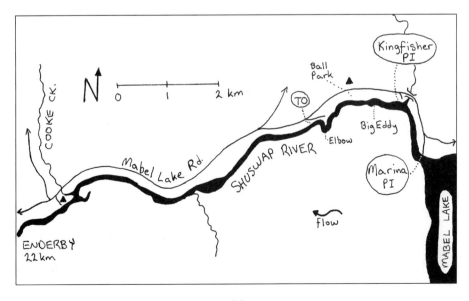

Adams River ⑱

Directions: From Kamloops, drive ~ 67 km East on Hwy. 1 past Chase and Little Shuswap Lake. On the Right, as you pass under Squilax bridge, will be signs pointing to Adams Lake, Anglemont, etc. (there are also signs for various resorts). Exit on the Right. From Salmon Arm, go ~ 44 km West on Hwy. 1 to this turn-off. From Vernon, the quickest highway route is probably via Salmon Arm on Hwys. 97A and 97B.

Sometimes swimming is easier than portaging the Gorge

To Take-Out: From the exit off Hwy. 1 drive 4.5 km to a bridge over the Adams. Cross the bridge and park on the Right. There are outhouses at the far end of the parking lot.

To Put-In: Turn around and drive back over the bridge 0.5 km and turn Right onto Holding Rd. This leads to Adams Lake. To scout the Gorge, drive 2.3 km. At a tight left corner, park on the Right. Walk down a steep bank along the farthest downstream trail. For the put-in, continue up Holding Rd. ~ 5.7 km to an upside-down-S-bend. At the left curve, park in the pullout on the Right. If you come to a **Y**, you have gone too far. Walk down a trail ~ 100m to an obvious put-in above the Weir.

Character: Medium to large volume, occasionally braided, lots of riffles. Two moments of excitement on an otherwise beautiful learning river. The Weir, which is not an actual weir, it just resembles a broken one, is a quick II+ to III chute that can have a nice wave. The Gorge, which can be portaged through the trees on the Left up and over the bluff, is an energetic series of III to IV- waves in a small, curving canyon that ends in a large pool.

Considerations: Sweepers and logs jams. Don't miss the take-out. The river below the take-out is very braided and is tangled with sweepers, strainers and log jams. There are signs that say people have gone for the eternal swim here.

Season: April to October. Biggest in June from snow-melt. Late July and August are best.

Class: II mostly. The river is not very challenging except at the Weir (II+ to III) and the Gorge (IV- at high water)

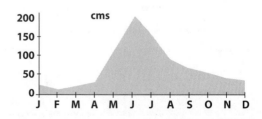

Length of Run: ~ 9 km.

Shuttle: ~ 8.5 km.

Camping:
▲ Shuswap Lake Prov. Park (Scotch Creek). Large site on the north shore of Shuswap Lake ~ 12 km past the take-out. Free hot showers. Reservations accepted.
▲ Frank's Campground across from ↑. Large, many amenities. 1 888 373-6151.

Free Camping: This area is under pressure from many groups who want to claim it as theirs. Therefore, not a lot of free space is available. If you do not see a 'No Camping' sign, try it.

Lodgings:
✔ Chase Visitor Info (250) 679-8432, email chccom@mail.ocis.net
✔ Scotch Creek Visitor Info (250) 955-2113, 1-888-955-1488 (toll free) www.shuswap.bc.ca/sunny/norshu,

Food & Drink: Groceries, restaurants and pubs are in Chase and at some spots along Shuswap Lake, including Scotch Creek.

Other Activities: *Watch salmon spawn and die. In October, and especially on every fourth year (the next one is 2002), the river comes alive with death. Access is a short drive past the take-out. You may even see a black bear loading up for hibernation. *Hike the historic Flume trails 5.2 km up on Holding Rd. The road to the parking lot is on the left of a tight right corner that just precedes a bridge over Hiuihill (Bear) Creek.

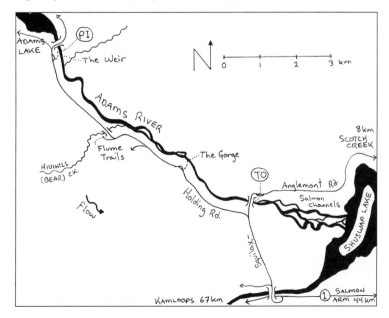

Barriere River

(and North Barriere River **CLASS III-** *)*

These two rivers can be run together or separately. Together it is a long run (~ 22.5 km), with the most difficult sections on the Barriere.

Directions: From Kamloops, follow Hwy. 5 (Yellowhead) North ~ 60 km. At Barriere Town Road (marked on the highway as Business Frontage Rd.) turn Right. Drive to the bridge over the Barriere River. From points north, follow Hwy. 5 South. Just past the bridge over the North Thompson River, turn Left onto Barriere Lake Rd. When at Barriere Town Rd., turn Right to the bridge.

To Take-Out:
- For the Barriere, see Directions. The bridge over the Barriere is the take-out.
- For the North Barriere take-out, continue along the paved Barriere Lake Rd. ~ 16 km until the road crosses the North Barriere. You can take-out and put-in beside the bridge, or just past the bridge, on the Left, is a small dirt road that leads to the river just upstream from the bridge.

To Put-In:
- For the Barriere, see North Barriere take-out.
- For the North Barriere, continue past the bridge ~ 5 km, following the signs to North Barriere Lake on gravel. The first bridge you cross is the put-in.

Character: The water is clear and warm, not pushy. At high water there are many waves, boofs and holes. Medium water offers up boulders. The Barriere begins and ends flat, but has a long boulder or hole garden in the middle that would be no fun to swim. The North Barriere is shorter and less difficult than the Barriere. The top 2/3 is continuous, the bottom is calm.

Considerations: Be careful of sweepers and logjams.

Season: Short. June is best but it can be possible from May to July.

Class: Barriere: II to III+. North Barriere: II to III at high water.

Length of Run: Barriere: 17 km or 2.5 hours. North Barriere: 5.5 km or 1 hour with play but no stops.

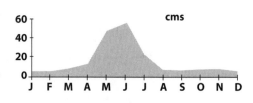

Shuttle: Total: ~ 21 km. Barriere: 16 km. North Barriere: 5 km.

Camping: There are Forestry sites at North, East and South Barriere Lakes. Fees were unclear, but probably free with the $27 pass, or $8 per night.

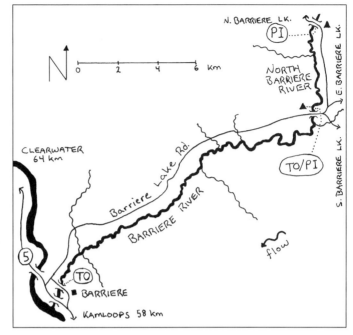

Free Camping:

▲ At the North Barriere takeout, follow the small dirt road that leads to the river. Here are a few small sites.

▲ At the North Barriere put-in, on the south-west side of the bridge are small sites in the open and in the trees.

Lodgings: There is no Visitor Info in Barriere. The closest is in Kamloops (250) 374-3377, 1 800 662-1994 (toll free) www.city.kamloops.bc.ca

Food & Drink: Groceries, restaurants and pubs are in Barriere.

Other Activities: The mountain biking in Kamloops and at Sun Peaks Resort is world-class. Contact Full Boar (250) 314-1888, Java Cycle (250) 314-5282 or Spoke & Motion (250) 372-3001 in Kamloops or Sun Peaks Resort (250) 578-7222.

Boofing on the Barriere

Clearwater River
In General

The Clearwater really has two sections separated by a long stretch of Class V+ rapids called the Kettle. Experts can combine the two runs with some slick paddling. Others can combine them with a long portage. This section covers general information about the river. The following sections deal with Above the Kettle and Below the Kettle. If you do wish to portage, use the instructions for the Above the Kettle take-out and the Below the Kettle put-in. It is a walk of ~ 1 km, or you may wish to use a third shuttle vehicle.

Directions: From Kamloops, follow Hwy. 5 North (Yellowhead) 130 km to the town of Clearwater. At the bottom of a hill, turn Left towards the town (follow the rafting signs). Drive 1.3 km to a bridge over the Clearwater. See the following sections for further information.

Camping:
▲ North Thompson BC Park at the confluence of the N. Thompson and Clearwater rivers. 4 km south of Clearwater off Hwy. 5. Outhouses.
▲ Spahats Creek in Wells Gray Prov. Park. Follow Clearwater Valley Rd. (on the opposite shore of the river from the put-in access road) ~ 15 km north of Clearwater.
▲ Dutch Lake Resort and RV Park near the take-out in town. Free showers. 1 888 884-4424, email: dlresort@mail.wellsgray.net

Free Camping: There are many side roads all along River Rd. Nothing much beside the river except at the take-out for Above the Kettle.

Lodgings: Clearwater Visitor Info
(250) 674-2646, email: clwcof@mail.wellsgray.net

Food & Drink: Groceries, restaurants and pubs are in Clearwater.

Other Activities: Wells Gray Provincial Park (250) 851-3000 is a mountainous area which offers many hikes to do, lakes to canoe and falls to view.

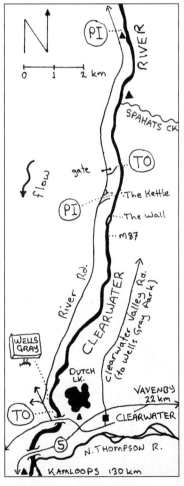

Clearwater River (20)
Above the Kettle

To Take-Out: From the bridge over the Clearwater, take an immediate Right onto Camp 2 Rd. Drive up Camp 2 Rd. for 0.7 km then take a hard Right onto the road with the sign for Wells Gray Provincial Park (although there is no road sign, the locals call this River Rd.). Drive 7.5 km on this brutally rough road to the Kettle. First you will see a gated road that leads down on the right. This is where Interior Whitewater puts its rafts in. Drive past this road just less than 1 km to a yellow gate. There is a pull-out on the Right and a small dirt road leading to the river. Park in the pullout. Walk down to the calm river so that you will know where to take-out.

To Put-In: Continue past the yellow gate ~ 5 km to a beach that can be seen through the trees when the road gets close to the river.

Character: Almost the entire run can be scouted from the road. Once you are downstream of Spahats Creek it gets

Most of the run is visible from the road

interesting with drops, holes and wave trains. The run begins placidly, then quickens, becomes wavy, then, if you don't take-out at the right place (see To Take-Out), it becomes crushing. Large volume.

Considerations: Don't miss the take-out, which is along a flat section. Just below it are the continuous, difficult rapids of the Kettle. These have been run in low water, but take a good long look before deciding to do so.

Season: May to October or November. Pounding huge in June. Best in the fall.

Class: III+ to IV+ at high water.

Length of Run: ~ 5 km.

Shuttle: ~ 5 km.

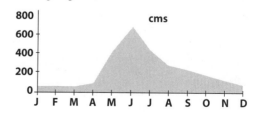

Clearwater River ㉑
Below the Kettle

To Take-Out: From the bridge over the Clearwater, take an immediate Right onto Camp 2 Rd. and park.

To Put-In: Continue up Camp 2 Rd. for 0.7 km then take a hard Right onto the road with the sign for Wells Gray Provincial Park (although there is no road sign, the locals call this River Rd.). Drive 7.5 km on this brutally rough road to the Kettle. First you will see a gated road that leads down on the right. This is where Interior Whitewater puts its rafts in. Drive past this road 100m until you come to a series of pull-outs. A trail leads down to many places where you can put-in. It is possible to maximize your run by putting in directly below the Kettle, which ends in a fast, constricted drop.

Character: This large-volume run begins with excitement then tapers off to flat water. First drops, then waves, then riffles. Immediately there are two islands dividing the river into three short channels. The middle one is the easiest but you can scout it before you put-in. Beyond that is The Wall, above another island that splits the river. We suggest running the left because there is often a glassy wave (The Wall) at the top. There is no eddy, so you must get it on the first try. The right is okay at low water, but be very careful. Then keep your eyes open for numerous waves.

Considerations: Behind the Wall can be very shallow - stay to the Right in the left channel. Just after, on the right, is M-87, a huge whirlpool at high water. Sheer canyon walls make up a large part of this run, so swims can be long. There are few options for walking out.

Season: May to October or November. Pounding huge in June. Best in the fall.

Class: III+ to IV+ at high water.

Length of Run: ~ 9 km.

Shuttle: ~ 8.5 km.

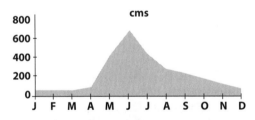

Below the Kettle at the put-in

Nicola River (22)

Directions: From Vancouver, drive Hwy. 1 North through the fabled Fraser Canyon and past the enticing big water of the Thompson. At Spences Bridge follow signs to Hwy. 8 towards Merritt. Use the Old Bridge as a distance reference point. You will soon be following the Nicola. If you come from Merritt, drive towards Spences Bridge on Hwy. 8. At ~ 5 km will be a **T** where Hwy. 97C joins. Use this **T** as a distance reference point.

As the road follows the river, there are plenty of put-ins and take-outs. The following are the more accessible:

To Take-Out:
- The Bridges: ~ 3.5 km from Old Bridge. They are very close to one another, so they can't be mistaken. The take-out is on river Right of the first bridge, or river Left of the second.
- Below Red Rock Canyon: ~ 15.2 km from Old Bridge, 41.8 km from **T**. Look for a large, flat area just downstream from the obvious canyon. There are two access roads.

To Put-In:
- Shackan campground: ~ 23.6 km from the Old Bridge, 33.4 km from **T**. There is a private bridge just upstream (for reference). In summer 2000, the campground did not appear to be operating.
- Below Red Rock Canyon: see 2nd take-out.

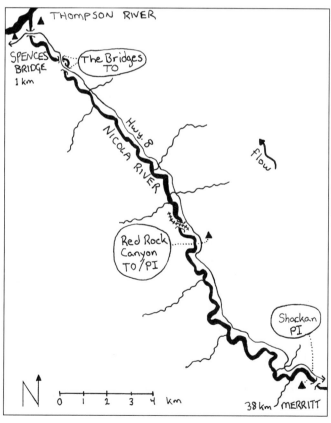

52

Character: Fun! The Nicola has easy passage around everything for novices, and lots of holes and waves for those looking for more challenge. After you enter Red Rock Canyon, the river takes a hard right. Stay to river right to avoid a large wave or hole (at high water) that is just around the corner in the main current on river left. At high water the river is energetic with almost continuous whitewater. At low water your bum will be bounced by rocks.

Considerations: Merritt treats its sewage before it enters the Nicola, but nutrients that pass through cows cling to the riverbed like a grey carpet after flood.

Season: The water can be a caramel washout in May and June; in a big year it floods farm fields upstream and washes down cow poop along with other debris. Later in July the water temperature warms up like a bath but it gets too low by mid-August.

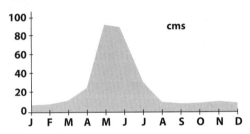

Class: II to II+ at high water.

Length of Run: ~ 25 km for full run. Shackan to Red Rock is about half that.

Shuttle:

Shackan	➜	Below Red Rock Canyon: 8.4 km
	➜	Bridges: 20 km
Red Rock	➜	Bridges: 11.7 km

Camping:
▲ BC Parks Cal Woods Recreation Reserve on the Thompson River along Hwy. 8 from Spences Bridge. There is a donation box for fees and facilities include outhouses, garbage cans and a message board.
▲ N'kwala Forestry campground is ~ 18 km East of Shackan put-in.
▲ 5 Nations campground at Curnow Bridge near the mouth of the Nicola. When we were there in May 2000 we couldn't determine its status - it didn't appear to be open or closed. If you stay there it would make for an ideal take-out.
▲ Acacia Grove RV park is across the Thompson River on the Spences Bridge side.

Free Camping:
▲ There are free sites along the river, but you will have to check these yourself. Any side road without a "No Trespassing" or similar sign is a good bet.
▲ Below Red Rock Canyon put-in / take-out serves well as a campground.
▲ Shackan campground at the put-in, although someone may come along for money in the 'high season'.

Camping beside the caramel at flood

Lodgings: Merritt Visitor Info (250) 378-2281, email: devofficer@city.merritt.bc.ca

Food & Drink: Groceries, restaurants and pubs are in Merritt. Spences Bridge is very small, but it has a pub and restaurant.

Other Activities: Catch (and release…) a trout or three in (one of) the trout capital(s) of the world. There is no lack of fishing, and information about it, all around Kamloops. Contact Merritt Visitor Info (above) or Kamloops Visitor Info (250) 374-3377, 1 800 662-1994 (toll free) www.city.kamloops.bc.ca

Info: Cal Woods campground has a message board if you need to leave a message for paddling partners.

Thompson River
In General

The Thompson is the classic big water river for southwestern BC. The river can be divided into two sections: an easier Above the Canyon and a more difficult Canyon, or they can be run together for a long day. The following sections explain each run.

Directions: From Vancouver, follow Hwy. 1 East to Hope. From there, continue up the Fraser Canyon on Hwy. 1 East for 116 km to Lytton. From Kamloops, follow Hwy. 1 West 135 km to Spences Bridge. Spences Bridge is at the north end (put-in) of the complete run. Lytton is at the south end (take-out).

Camping:
- ▲ Skihist BC Park is ~ 8 km east of Lytton on Hwy. 1. The campground is on the uphill (south) side of the highway. A picnic area is on the other side.
- ▲ Goldpan BC Park is ~ 9 km south of Spences Bridge on Hwy. 1. This site is on the river.
- ▲ There are two commercial RV parks just south of Lytton on Hwy. 1, and one to the east.

Free Camping: This area is within a massive canyon; therefore, there is not a lot of room to camp in. Most flat spaces have been spoken for. There are side roads to try, but some are gated.

Lodgings: Lytton Visitor Info (250) 455-2523, email: lyttoncc@goldtrail.com

Food & Drink: Groceries, restaurants and pubs are in Lytton. Spences Bridge is very small, but it has a pub and restaurant.

Other Activities: Hike the Stein Valley (Nlaka'pamux Heritage Prov. Park). You may also want to carry your boat up the trail after you scout it. From Lytton cross the Thompson on Hwy. 12 towards Lillooet. You will soon come to the free ferry across the Fraser. Take it, then continue north ~ 6 km to the entrance to the Stein.

In the belly of the Canyon

Thompson River (23)
Above the Canyon

To Take-Out: From Lytton, drive ~ 16 km on Hwy. 1 East to Nicaomen Creek. Just before the railroad overpass park on the Right. If this lot is full, continue under the RR overpass and park on the Right. From Spences Bridge, drive south ~ 19.5 on Hwy. 1 to Nicaomen Creek. Drive beneath the railroad overpass and immediately park on your Left. If this lot is full, turn around and again drive beneath the RR overpass and park on your Right.

To Put-In: From the take-out, follow Hwy. 1 East ~ 14.5 km to a pull-off on the Left across from Bighorn sand shed. This put-in is ~ 5 km south of Spences Bridge (~ 4 km north of Goldpan Prov Park).

Character: Big, powerful water, although mostly flat. If you have no experience with huge volume you may wish to get your feet (or at least hands and face) wet here. There are some waves, eddy lines and boils to practice on that are unlike any tiny creek. If you aren't balanced in the boils you will have plenty of opportunity to practice your roll. And failing that, the water is nice and warm for swimming (at least in late summer).

Considerations: Volume! Don't miss the take-out if you aren't ready for the next challenge - the Canyon!

Season: All year. August and September are ideal. Spring runoff can be ugly with the amount of water, mud and debris.

Class: II to II+ at high water.

Length of Run: ~ 15 km.

Shuttle: ~ 14.5 km.

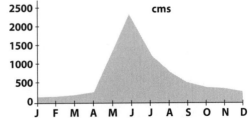

56

Thompson River
The Canyon

To Take-Out: At the town of Lytton, exit Hwy. 1. Follow signs to Lillooet via Hwy. 12. Cross the bridge over the Thompson and park. In the summer of 2000 a new bridge was being built so we are not sure of what parking will be available. Just down the highway there is a gated road that leads ~ 200m to the confluence of the Thompson and Fraser rivers. For $2 per kayak (payable to the local Indian band) you can drive down to the river.

To Put-In: Back on Hwy. 1 East, drive ~ 16 km to Nicaomen Creek. Just before the railroad overpass park on the Right. If this lot is full, continue under the RR overpass and park on the Right. From the first lot, cross the highway (luckily traffic is usually travelling slowly here) and walk upstream 50 m to where a ramp has been built to lower rafts.

Character: Powerful! Big! There are glassy waves (one of some renown at the top of the Frog, which is the first feature below the put-in), wave trains, violent laterals and strong, squirrelly boils. More interesting play spots arise with the lowering of the river. The run is not continuous whitewater, but breaks never last long. The most difficult rapids are in the first half. A strong head wind almost always kicks up in the afternoon, so save some energy for paddling, or go early.

Considerations: When in doubt or fear, stay Left. This is particularly true for Cutting Board Drop, shortly after the Frog. When you see a rock island in the middle of the river, choose Left. It is possible to scout this from the highway if you park carefully.

Season: All year. August and September are ideal. Spring runoff can be ugly with the amount of water, mud and debris.

Class: III+ to IV. The features are not difficult to paddle, but the sheer volume of water can have its way with you.

Length of Run: ~ 16.5 km.

Shuttle: ~ 17km.

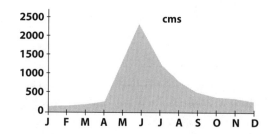

The Frog

Nahatlatch River
In General

This section covers general information about Between the Lakes, Frances Lake to the Canyon, and the Canyon. Following are sections which explain each run specifically. We recommend combining Frances Lake to the Canyon and the Canyon as the former is a good warm-up for the latter, at least at low water. In fact, all three can be combined with a kilometer of flatwater paddling across Frances Lake.

Directions: From Vancouver, drive on Hwy. 1 East to Hope. From there, continue up the Fraser Canyon on Hwy. 1 East for ~ 70 km to Boston Bar. Turn Left off the highway. From Kamloops or points north, follow Hwy. 1 West to Lytton. From Lytton, continue ~ 47 km on Hwy. 1 West to Boston Bar and turn Right off the highway. Drive down the hill and turn Right at the **Y** towards North Bend. Cross the bridge over the Fraser. From here, drive ~ 16 km (the first 8 km is paved) to the bridge over the Nahatlatch (which we will call the Bridge). From here, refer to the individual run sections.

Camping:
- ▲ Apocynum FS site. At the put-in for the Canyon / take-out for Frances Lake. ~ 3.1 km from the Bridge. $27 Pass or $8. 6 - 7 sites. Outhouse.
- ▲ Fir Flat FS site. At the other put-in for the Canyon / take-out for Frances Lake. ~ 1.6 km past Apocynum. Pass or $8. Tiny. Outhouse.
- ▲ Log Creek FS site. ~ 6 km past Fir Flat. Pass or $8. Small. Outhouse. Message board.
- ▲ Frances Lake BC Park. At the put-in. East end of the lake, one site, outhouse.
- ▲ Old Ranger Station BC Park. ~ 2.7 km west of Frances Lake put-in. Two sites, outhouse.
- ▲ Salmon Beach BC Park. ~ 4.7 km past Old Ranger. One site, outhouse.
- ▲ Nahatlatch River FS site. ~ 1.5 km before the Bridge (coming from North Bend), turn Left at the **Y**. Drive ~ 5 to 7 km (this is a guess). This site is on the opposite side of the Nahatlatch, but could be used as a put-in for the Canyon.
- ▲ Alexandra Bridge BC Park. ~ 22 km south of Boston Bar on Hwy. 1.

Free Camping: There are side roads all along the river that lead to the water. The further up you go the more private property there is.

Lodgings:
- ✔ Yale Visitor Info (604) 863-2324.
- ✔ Lytton Visitor Info (250) 455-2523, email: lyttoncc@goldtrail.com
- ✔ Hope Visitor Info (604) 869-2021, email: hopechmb@uniserve.com
  www.hopechamber.bc.ca

Food & Drink: Boston Bar is a very small community. Some services exist, but Hope and Lytton are the closest towns of any size.

Other Activities:

What else could you want to do? This is one of the best river runs around. Well, if you must: Hike down to Hell's Gate on the Fraser River, ~ 12 km south of Boston Bar on Hwy 1. You can, of course, take the tram,

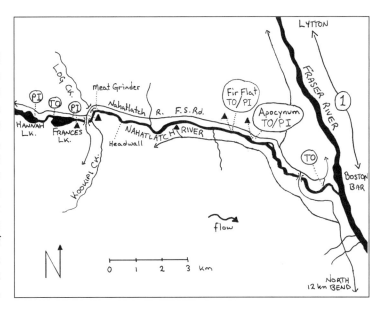

but the hike is only ~ 1.5 km round-trip which is good for loosening up the legs. You will find the footpath (actually a gravel road) just South of the foot-traffic overpass. Take the opportunity to scout one of the largest river features in the province.

Info: ~ 1 km upstream from the Bridge is a water level information board sponsored by REO Rafting.

The Canyon

Nahatlatch River ㉕

Between the Lakes

To Take-Out: From the bridge over the Nahatlatch (ie. the Bridge), drive ~ 12.5 km to the west end of Frances Lake. Look for a pullout where the river empties into Frances.

To Put-In: Drive ~ 0.8 km further until you come to a campsite at the east end of Hannah Lake. Park on the Right.

Character: A very short warm-up for the lower sections. A shallow class III boulder garden.

Considerations: Look out for sweepers. Don't blink or you may miss the run.

Season: May to October. Big water in June.

Class: III.

Length of Run: ~ 1 km.

Shuttle: ~ 0.8 km.

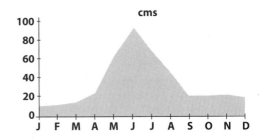

Preparing for the day

Nahatlatch River

Frances Lake to The Canyon

The road follows the river so there are numerous places to put-in and take-out. The following are the most common:

To Take-Out:

✦ From the Bridge over the Nahatlatch, drive upstream for ~ 3.1 km until you come to Apocynum FS Rec site. Drive to the end of the site where you can park beside the river.

✦ Fir Flat FS Rec site is 1.6 km further up the road, sandwiched between the road and river.

To Put-In: Back on the road, continue upstream ~ 8 km (from Apocynum) until you come to a **Y** just past Log Ck. FS Rec site. (Before this site, at the 23 km sign, you can view Meat Grinder from the road.) At the **Y**, turn Right and drive a further 0.5 km to Frances Lake just inside the BC Park boundary. The put-in is at Frances Lake Rec site.

Character: Medium volume. Around the first bend is a rock garden that ends in Meat Grinder, a IV to IV+ drop that is just around the second bend. A second drop, Headwall, III+ to IV-, is ~ 1 km downstream and bends left. After this the river mellows until a boulder or hole garden near the take-outs. Waves, holes, boofs, everything. Bony at low water, some braiding.

Considerations: Watch for log jams and sweepers.

Season: May to October.

Class: III+ with two harder drops (see Character).

Length of Run: ~ 8.5 km for full run.

Shuttle: ~ 9 km for full run.

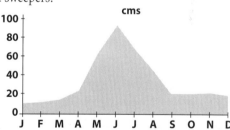

Hammin' it 'n' jammin' it

Nahatlatch River ㉗
The Canyon

To Take-Out: Cross the Bridge, drive ~ 100 m and take a Right off the main road. This road goes downstream towards the Fraser. ~ 1.5 km down, past some driveways, is a **Y**. Turn Right and follow the road to a large eddy on the Nahatlatch. Don't miss this take-out as the most difficult drop of the run is just below. And hiking back up afterwards is brutal.

To Put-In:
- Return to the main road and continue upstream for ~ 3 km until you come to Apocynum FS Rec site. Drive to the end of the site where you can park beside the river.
- Fir Flat FS Rec site is 1.6 km further up the road, sandwiched between the road and river.

Character: At high water this run roars. From the REO rafting base on the left bank, the river becomes a mad rush of wild water as it enters a gorgeous canyon that twists, turns and crashes its way down to the take-out. About halfway there is a nasty class V that can be scouted and portaged on the Left. At low water this canyon becomes very entertaining pool-drop.

Considerations: Scout this sucker if it's your first time! The channels can get very narrow. At low water watch for boulders in the drops.

Season: Late April to October. Best after melt, in July and August. Safest later.

Class: Relentless IV+ to V in high water. III+ to IV in low water. The V drop is always a V.

Length of Run: ~ 5 km from Apocynum.

Shuttle: ~ 4.3 km.

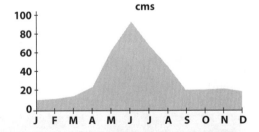

Entering the fray at low water

Bridge River ㉘

Directions: From Vancouver, drive along Hwy. 99 North via Whistler to Lillooet, or else take Hwy. 1 East then Hwy. 12 North at Lytton to Lillooet. From Kamloops, follow Hwy. 1 West to Cache Creek, then Hwy. 97 North briefly to the Hwy. 99 turnoff. From there continue to Lillooet.

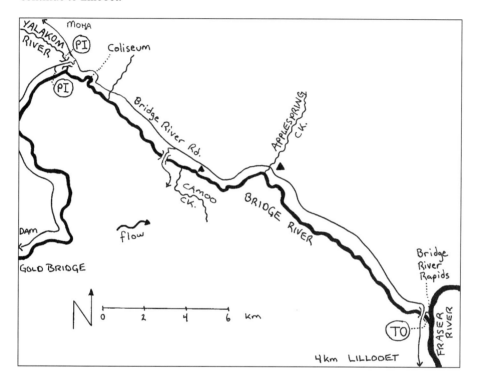

To Take-Out:
↗ Drive north all the way through the town of Lillooet. Just before you reach Old Mill Plaza, turn Left onto Bridge River Rd., following signs towards Gold Bridge, Seton Portage, etc. Travel ~ 6 km to the take-out bridge over the Bridge. Just up the road you can see the last drop, a river-wide fanning ledge.

∅ Camoo Creek has been closed to public access. If you have a really convincing argument for using it you may get a sympathetic hearing. Bridge River Indian Band (250) 256-7423.

To Put-In:
↖ Continue to follow the road ~ 22 km to a stunning view of the river as it performs in the Coliseum. From there it is another 3.5 km to the bridge over the Yalakom River. There are thin shoulders to park on around the bridge (or you may want to ask

Playing the slots

the nearby homeowner if he would tolerate your vehicle for the day). Put-in on the Yalakom beside the bridge.

✦ ~ 0.5 km further there is a steep, short, gravel road on the Left that goes down to the Bridge River. In July 2000 this was a very shallow put-in.

Character: A river-running special. Pool-drops, boofs galore, and conglomerate boulder gardens from a fantasy. The beginning (above, in and below the Coliseum), middle (a series of three ledges and a house rock ~ 2 km past Camoo Ck. bridge) and end (conglomerate boulder gardens and slots) all perform with flourish. Between these acts are plenty of opportunities to practice your stroke.

Considerations: Scout for logs in the tight channels (some ~ 1 m wide). Be careful of broaching.

Season: May to September. We paddled it when the water was up to the vegetation level - ideal! The Bridge is currently undergoing some flow changes at the hands of its human managers. The upper Bridge flows into Carpenter Lake, which is then drained through tunnels to drive generators at Seton Portage. As a result, in the past, no water left the lake through the lower Bridge. However, as of summer 2000, BC Hydro, through pressure from The Department of Fisheries and Oceans and the Ministry of the Environment, is once again releasing water from Carpenter Lake into Bridge River to reestablish salmon spawning habitat. The amount of water, though, is

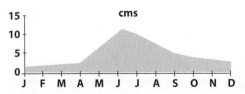

very small and will barely affect the overall flow of the section described here. The run described here is mostly contributed by the Yalakom River.

Class: IV.

Length of Run: ~ 26 km. 5 - 7 hours.

Shuttle: ~ 25.5 km.

Camping: Cayoosh Creek Park campground. In the town of Lillooet, it is below the Fraser River bridge.

Free Camping:
▲ Seton Dam campground (BC Hydro) is a large site just west of the canal bridge at the south end of Lillooet on Hwy. 99. Outhouses and firewood.
▲ Applespring Creek is a very small site beside the road ~ 11 km past the take-out.
▲ There is a bench above the river that offers a number of flat spots. It is the first Left after Applespring, ~ 4 km.

Lodgings: Lillooet Visitor Info (250) 256-4308.

Food & Drink: Lillooet has a large grocery store at the north end of town. There are restaurants and pubs in the downtown.

Other Activities: View the Bridge River rapids on the Fraser River. From the take-out bridge, find a path on the northeast side. Walk among the spectacular rocks and native fishing grounds until you reach a point where the Fraser is raising hell during flood.

Below Camoo Creek

Cayoosh Creek (29)

Directions: From Vancouver, drive along Hwy. 99 North via Whistler to Lillooet, or else take Hwy. 1 East then Hwy. 12 North at Lytton to Lillooet. From Kamloops, follow Hwy. 1 West to Cache Creek, then Hwy. 97 North briefly to the Hwy. 99 turnoff. From there, continue to Lillooet. From Lillooet, follow Hwy. 99 South towards Pemberton. You will soon cross a bridge that spans a BC Hydro canal. Use this spot as your measuring reference point.

If you come via Whistler, you will be backwards. The first put-in is ~ 65 km from the intersection at Mt. Currie. You can figure out the rest of the math.

To Take-Out: From the canal bridge, drive ~ 14 km to a bridge on your Right that crosses Cayoosh. Park at the bridge.

To Put-In:

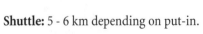 Continue on Hwy. 99 ~ 4 km until you see Cottonwood FS Campground. Drive ~ 1 kilometer further until you reach the end of a straight stretch that then bends left. Before the curve, look for a small gravel road with a parking lot on your Right.

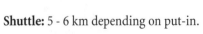 For a more challenging start to your paddle, continue ~ 1 km until you see a dirt road on your Right. It curves around to the left and meets up again with the highway. Just before it does so, park. The put-in is down a grassy bank where the two roads meet.

Character: Straight-forward, quick, shallow, waves, a few holes.

Considerations: Be careful of sweepers and logs. High water washes out most eddies.

Season: May to August.

Class: From the 1st put-in: II+. From the 2nd put-in to the 1st: III.

Length of Run: 5 - 6 km depending on put-in. About 1 hour.

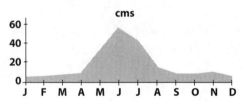

Shuttle: 5 - 6 km depending on put-in.

Camping:
- ▲ Cinnamon FS campground. ~ 1 km South of the take-out. Outhouses. $27 pass or $8/night. Good for a take-out if staying.
- ▲ Cottonwood FS campground. See directions to the 1st put-in. Outhouses. $27 pass or $8/night.
- ▲ Cayoosh Creek Park campground. In the town of Lillooet, it is below the Fraser River bridge.

Free Camping:
- ▲ Seton Dam campground (BC Hydro) is a large site just West of the canal bridge. Outhouses and firewood.
- ▲ There are a number of decent sites beside the river. Try any road that doesn't have a discouraging sign.

Lodgings: Lillooet Visitor Info
(250) 256-4308.

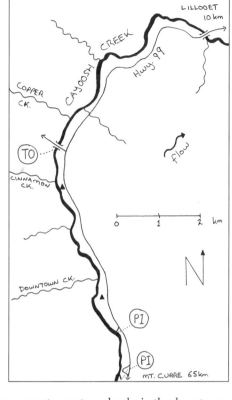

Food & Drink: Lillooet has a large grocery store at the north end of town. There are restaurants and pubs in the downtown.

Other Activities: Try to surf the discharge into Seton Lake at the BC Hydro Seton Lake Rec. Site. You probably aren't supposed to, but it's a good challenge.

Hey, the fence isn't in the water!

CLASS III+

Birkenhead River ③⓪

A typical stretch; none too punishing

Directions: From Vancouver, follow Hwy. 99 North via Whistler to Mount Currie. It is about a 3 hour trip. From Lillooet, drive for 2 hours along Hwy. 99 South to Mount Currie.

To Take-Out: From Mount Currie, drive North towards D'Arcy. Immediately before the railway tracks, turn Right. Follow this gravel road ~ 1 km to a foot bridge over the Birkenhead.

To Put-In: Return to the main road, cross the tracks and continue north. Drive ~ 6 km to the first bridge crossing the river.

Character: Wide, shallow, continuous waves. Small rock and boulder gardens. Technical when small, lots of breaking water when high.

Considerations: Watch for sweepers and log jams.

Season: May to early August. Also the fall if the rain falls.

Class: III+

Length of Run: ~ 5 km.

Shuttle: ~ 7 km.

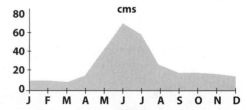

Camping:
▲ Owl Creek FS Rec site is ~ 4 km north of the railroad tracks.
▲ Spetch Creek FS Rec site is ~ 5 km north of the put-in.
▲ Nairn Falls BC Park is ~ 3 km south of Pemberton on Hwy. 99.

Free Camping: If it doesn't say 'No Camping', try it.

Lodgings: Pemberton Visitor Info (604) 894-6175 or 894-6477   www.pemberton.net

Food & Drink: Groceries, restaurants and pubs are in Mt. Currie and Pemberton.

Other Activities: Explore Joffre Lakes Provincial Park. Get up close and personal with glaciers ~ 25 km east of Mt. Currie off Hwy. 99 (Duffy Lake Rd.). The hike to the glaciers is along a 3 km trail with 3 lakes on the way.

Info: For current information, contact Captain Holiday's Kayak Adventure School (604) 905-2925 www.kayakwhistler.com

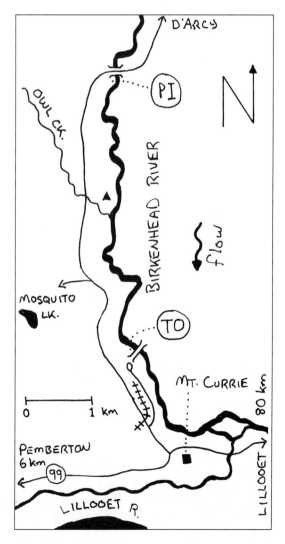

Lillooet River
In General

This section deals with general information regarding the Lillooet river north of Pemberton. Following are sections that deal specifically with Above Meager Creek and Below Meager Creek.

Directions: From Vancouver, follow Hwy. 99 North via Whistler to Pemberton. From Lillooet, follow Hwy. 99 South to Pemberton. Each route takes ~ 2.5 hours. From Pemberton, follow signs to Pemberton Meadows along Pemberton Valley Rd. When you have travelled ~ 27 km (where you will see a lonely telephone) turn Right, following signs to Goldbridge and Meager Ck. In ~ 1 km you will cross a bridge over the Lillooet, and will then be driving on the rough gravel Lillooet FS Rd. The kilometer markers start at 0. See the following sections for further instructions.

Camping: No one wants your money up this far, so if you insist on paying to sleep, check around Pemberton. See Lodgings for info.

Free Camping:
▲ At the 38 km marker on Lillooet FS Rd. (1 km past the intersection with Meager Creek Main) is a temporary Forest Service site. Down by the river is nice, but otherwise rather dismal (although good for large groups). Phone (604) 898-2100 to check its status. Outhouses.
▲ The parking spot for the Above Meager Creek put-in is an open site above the river.
▲ ~ 1 km past the Above Meager Creek put-in is a small sheltered site.
▲ If desperate, 0.4 km before the Below Meager Creek take-out is a small road on the river side of the road. It is unattractive and the flies were atrocious in early July, but it is sheltered.

Lodgings: Pemberton Visitor Info (604) 894-6175 or (604) 894-6477
www.pemberton.net

Food & Drink: Groceries, restaurants and pubs are in Pemberton.

Other Activities: Soak in one of two hot springs. *Meager Creek hot springs are day use only. Absolutely beautiful, they cost $5 per person per day. At the 37 km marker on Lillooet FS Rd., follow Meager Creek Main Rd. to the bridge over the Lillooet. Here you must pay an attendant. The springs are a further 7 km. They are subject to closure so phone (604) 898-2100 to check status. *Keyhole hot springs are free. Drive ~ 2 km past the put-in for Above Meager Creek to a creek that in July 2000 flowed across the road. From here you should see Keyhole Falls across the valley to your left. Find a path on the far side of the creek that crosses a bench then descends steeply to the Lillooet. Look for yellow ribbons. You

71

may want to bring a shovel so you can dig a pit in the hot mud that can then fill in with water.

Info: *For current information, contact Captain Holiday's Kayak Adventure School (604) 905-2925 www.kayakwhistler.com. * Ministry of Forests, Squamish District (604) 898-2100 has info on Meager Creek and its related campsite at 38 km.

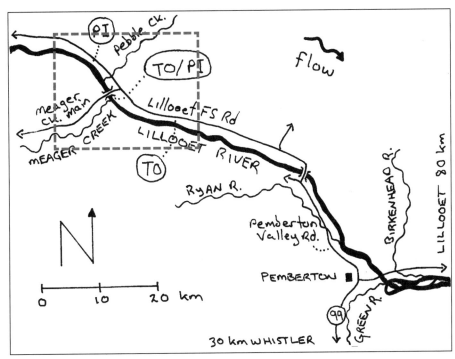

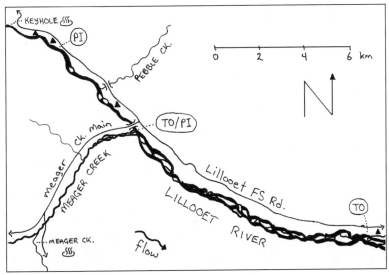

enlarged area inset of above map

Lillooet River
(31)
Above Meager Creek

To Take-Out: From the 0 km marker drive along Lillooet FS Rd. Before the 9 km marker is a **Y**, stay Left towards Meager Ck. At the 37 km marker is the intersection with Meager Creek Main Rd. Here there is a bridge over the Lillooet. This is the take-out.

To Put-In: Continue upstream on Lillooet FS Rd. You will soon cross Pebble Creek bridge. Travel ~ 3 km more and you will see where the road meets the river. Just past and up the hill is a good parking spot.

Character: Large volume. Big waves, boulder gardens, rock gardens, ice-cold, silty, continuous.

Considerations: The water is always silty, which makes it difficult to see things. Watch for logs. Don't swim, it's too cold.

Season: May to October. Begins with snow-melt, then glacier-melt, then rainfall.

Class: III to III+. Possibly IV at high water.

Length of Run: ~ 5 km.

Shuttle: ~ 4.5 km.

cms

400
300
200
100
0

J F M A M J J A S O N D

Keyhole hot springs hanging over the Lillooet

73

Lillooet River

(32)

Below Meager Creek

To Take-Out: From the 0 km marker drive along Lillooet FS Rd. Before the 9 km marker is a **Y**, stay Left towards Meager Ck. Just past the 24 km marker, where the road meets the river, is the take-out. Small parking spaces are on the right of the road.

To Put-In: Continue on the Lillooet FS Rd. until you reach the Meager Creek intersection at the 37 km marker. Here is a bridge over the Lillooet. This is the put-in.

Character: Braided, meandering, large volume, ice-cold.

Considerations: Constantly changing channels. The silty water makes it difficult to see things. Watch for log jams and sweepers on the sides. Too cold for swimming.

Season: May to October. Begins dropping in August.

Class: II. High water may increase to II+.

Length of Run: ~ 13 km.

Shuttle: ~ 13 km.

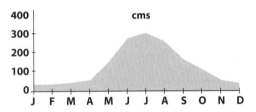

Soo River (33)

Directions: From Vancouver follow Hwy. 99 North to Whistler (~ 2 hrs). From Kamloops and points east, follow Hwy. 99 South from north of Cache Creek to Pemberton (~ 4.5 hrs from Kamloops).

To Take-Out: From Whistler Village, continue on Hwy. 99 ~ 20 km to a bridge over the Soo. Just before this bridge, on the Left, are two sites beside the river where you can park. From Pemberton, follow Hwy. 99 South ~ 9.7 km to just past the bridge over the Soo.

To Put-In: Drive upstream on Hwy. 99 ~ 2.8 km to where the highway, after a straight stretch, begins to climb and bend left. The small dirt road turnoff is on the Right as the bend begins. The narrow road ends in a turnaround. Before this turnaround is a path to the Right. Walk down this path until it begins to curve left and climb back uphill. At this point, turn Right and walk along an obscure path through the trees to the river.

Character: Technical, continuous pool-drops and boulder gardens. Small to medium volume. Bony in late summer (and fall if no rain). Pushy when it is running high. If the gravel bar at the take-out is submerged, the river if too high to run.

Considerations: Two drops should be scouted from shore. The first (and easier of the two) is about 1/3 of the way down. The second, Linda Lovelace, is about halfway down. Watch for logs and sweepers that may require a portage. Rock work being done on the railroad at the time of publication may change some rapids.

Season: All year is possible if the rains cooperate in the fall and winter. Spring

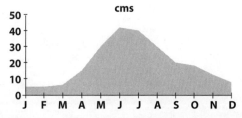

75

flood is a time for the experts. Late summer for the rest of us.

Class: IV to IV+ in high water.

Length of Run: ~ 3 km.

Shuttle: ~ 3 km.

Camping: Nairn Falls BC Park is ~ 3 km south of Pemberton on Hwy. 99.

Free Camping: In this part of the world, with its rapid tourism-fueled expansion, this section is too difficult to keep up with. Look around and if there is no sign saying 'No Camping', try it.

Lodgings:
✔ Whistler Visitor Info (604) 932-5528.
✔ Pemberton Visitor Info (604) 894-6175 or 894-6477 www.pemberton.net

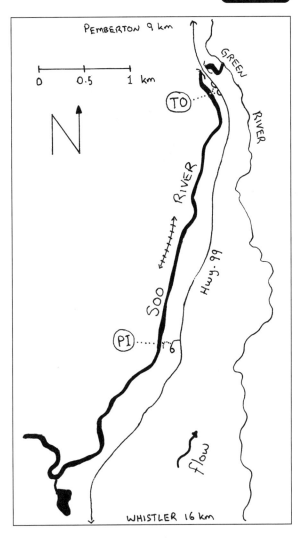

Food & Drink: Restaurants, pubs and groceries are in Whistler and Pemberton. Bring extra money.

Other Activities: *There is some great mountain biking in this area, including the Tour Du Soo. Contact Evolution (604) 932-2967 in Whistler. *Hike to Nairn Falls to see two impressive waterfalls - one of which drops into a natural tunnel - and some big rapids. See the Camping section for directions.

Info: For current information, contact Captain Holiday's Kayak Adventure School (604) 905-2925 www.kayakwhistler.com

Green River ㉞

Directions: This run is easiest to explain from Whistler. Therefore, from Vancouver, follow Hwy. 99 North ~ 2 hours to Whistler.

To Take-Out: From Whistler Village, continue along Hwy. 99 North ~ 12 km, passing Green Lake. Pass the (Garibaldi) Wedgemount turnoff and continue ~ 0.5 km. Here, on the right, is a small turnoff at the north end of the highway pylons. Follow the switchback to the railroad tracks. Park here and walk across the tracks to the river.

To Put-In: Back on Hwy. 99, drive south towards Whistler ~ 4.5 km

Precarious, hopeful scouting (Not Green River!...but near)

until you see the turn-off to Summer Lane, by Green Lake, on the Left. Then follow Summer Lane to the Left. At the end of this road is a boat launch.

Character: The approach across the north end of Green Lake is a good warm-up. A challenging river for beginners. Small volume. Pool-drops and boulder gardens. Technical when small, amongst the trees when high.

Considerations: Watch for sweepers and logs.

Season: Spring melt to August.

Class: II to III at high water.

Length of Run: ~ 5 km.

Shuttle: ~ 5 km.

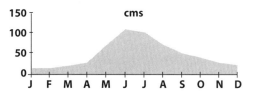

Camping:
▲ Brandywine Prov. Park campground at the north end of Daisy Lake. ~ 25 km south of Whistler Village on Hwy. 99 South. Small site. Outhouses.
▲ Nairn Falls BC Park is ~ 3 km south of Pemberton on Hwy. 99.

Free Camping: In this part of the world, with its rapid tourism-fueled expansion, this section is too difficult to keep up with. Look around and unless there is a sign saying 'No Camping', try it.

Lodgings: Whistler Visitor Info (604) 932-5528.

Food & Drink: Restaurants, pubs and groceries are in Whistler. Bring extra money.

Other Activities: Whistler/Blackcomb resort (604) 932-3141 offers year-round activities including summer mountain biking and glacier skiing / snowboarding.

Info: For current information, contact Captain Holiday's Kayak Adventure School (604) 905-2925 www.kayakwhistler.com

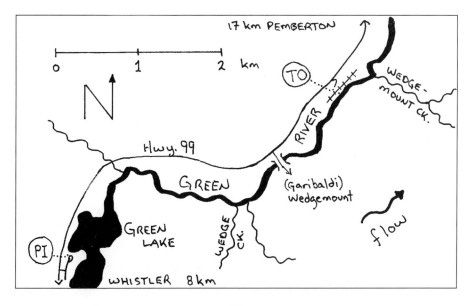

Cheakamus River (35)
Upper

non-ferocious autumn paddling

Directions: From Vancouver, follow Hwy. 99 North towards Whistler. ~ 8 km before Whistler Village (4 km before Creekside) you will arrive at Function Junction, the industrial end of Whistler. Turn Right towards Cheakamus Lake. From points north and east via Pemberton, follow Hwy. 99 South towards and past Whistler. ~ 8 km south of Whistler (4 km after Creekside) turn Left towards Cheakamus Lake.

To Take-Out: Follow the paved road across the bridge over the Cheakamus (ie. Don't follow the dirt road on the left to Cheakamus Lake). This is the take-out. Park ~ 30m upstream past the bridge where you see the Cheakamus West FS Rd bears Left (this road also has a blue sign that says 'Westside Main - kayak access points'). On the Left is a parking lot. ~ 1.5 km down, past other possible take-outs, is a Class VI falls that you really don't want to go down ☠.

To Put-In:
- Continue ~ 1km up Cheakamus W. FS Rd. where you will see another blue sign that reads 'kayak put-ins' pointing Left. Down this road is a parking lot. Walk upstream to find a put-in.
- Continue another 1 km up Cheakamus W. FS Rd., past a big hill, until you reach a small pullout on the Left. The river is adjacent. If you find yourself in over your head, you can use above the 1st put-in as a take-out.

Character: Short, continuous pool-drop. Technical, fast water. Small volume. Plenty of channels, walls and corners. Very pushy at higher levels, really a different river all together.

Considerations: Scout ahead for fallen logs (see Other Activities).

79

Season: From May to October. June and July are high water. September is good because the flood madness has sub-sided. The volume of water is approximately ¹/₂ that below Daisy Lake.

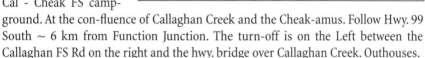

Class: Low water: IV-. High water: IV+.

Length of Run: 1.3 km for the short run. ~ 2.5 km for the full run.

Shuttle: ~ 1 km for the short run. ~ 2 km for the full run.

Camping:
▲ Cal - Cheak FS campground. At the con-fluence of Callaghan Creek and the Cheak-amus. Follow Hwy. 99 South ~ 6 km from Function Junction. The turn-off is on the Left between the Callaghan FS Rd on the right and the hwy. bridge over Callaghan Creek. Outhouses.
▲ Brandywine Prov. Park campground at the north end of Daisy Lake. ~ 25 km south of Whistler Village on Hwy. 99 South. Small site. Outhouses.

Free Camping:
▲ In this part of the world, with its rapid tourism-fueled expansion, this section is too difficult to keep up with. Look around and unless there is a sign saying 'No Camping', try it.
▲ The lower Cheakamus river has many free sites beside it. Please refer to the section on the Cheakamus: Paradise Valley.

Lodgings: Whistler Visitor Info (604) 932-5528.

Food & Drink: Groceries, pubs and restaurants are in Whistler. Nothing comes cheap.

Other Activities: Scout the river by following Riverside Trail on the south side of the river (ie. On the upstream side of the take-out bridge). It should largely be called Withinearshotoftheriver Trail, but all major drops have little paths to them. This trail connects the take-out and the two put-ins.

Info: For current information, contact Captain Holiday's Kayak Adventure School (604) 905-2925 www.kayakwhistler.com.

Cheakamus River (36)
Below Daisy Lake

The view from Alpine bridge

Directions: From Vancouver, follow Hwy. 99 North to Squamish. From the traffic lights at Cleveland Ave., continue north ~ 28 km to the take-out. From Whistler, drive ~ 27 km on Hwy. 99 South to the highway bridge over the Cheakamus just below the Daisy Lake dam (this is the put-in).

To Take-Out: From the bridge below Daisy Lake, drive south ~ 4 km along Hwy. 99 to a large pull-off on the west side of the road. The river is adjacent. From Squamish, if you cross the bridge below Daisy Lake, then you have gone ~ 4 km too far. ☺

To Put-In:
- Drive ~ 4 km north on Hwy. 99 (keep your eyes open for Alpine bridge on your Left so that you can scout the IV to IV+ drop) until you come to the bridge that crosses the Cheakamus just below the dam. There is room for one small car on the southeast side of the bridge.
- Otherwise, drive back downstream ~200 m to the first road on the Left, park there and walk back to the 1st put-in. This road leads to the Garibaldi Lake (Black Tusk) trailhead.

Character: Medium volume. Boulder gardens and pool-drops. Continuous action. Technical when low, lots of waves when high. One large IV to IV+ drop that can be scouted beforehand from Alpine bridge about half way down.

Considerations: Be careful of broken tree stumps below water level.

Season: May to September, but best in the middle of the summer.

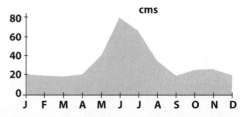

Class: III (III+ at high water) with one IV (IV+) drop.

Length of Run: ~ 4 km.

Shuttle: ~ 3.5 km.

Camping:
▲ Cal - Cheak FS campground. At the confluence of Callaghan Creek and the Cheakamus. Follow Hwy. 99 South ~ 14 km from Whistler. The turn-off is on the Left between the Callaghan FS Rd on the right and the hwy. bridge over Callaghan Creek. Outhouses.
▲ Alice Lake Provincial Park campground. $18.50 per site. ~ 10 km north of the Cleveland Ave. lights in Squamish, or ~ 19 km south of the take-out.
▲ Brandywine Prov. Park campground at the north end of Daisy Lake. ~ 25 km south of Whistler Village on Hwy. 99 South. Small site. Outhouses.

Free Camping:
▲ In this part of the world, with its rapid tourism-fueled expansion, this section is too difficult to keep up with. Look around and unless there is a sign saying 'No Camping', try it.
▲ The lower Cheakamus river has many free sites beside it. Please refer to the section on the Cheakamus: Paradise Valley.

Lodgings:
✔ Squamish Visitor Info (604) 892-9244, email: information@squamishchamber.bc.ca www.squamishchamber.bc.ca
✔ Whistler Visitor Info (604) 932-5528.

Food & Drink: Groceries, restaurants and pubs are in Squamish and Whistler.

Other Activities: Hike to Garibaldi Lake in Garibaldi Prov. Park. For a stunning view of - and access to - the Coastal mountains (including Black Tusk, a volcanic spire), hike ~ 3 to 4 hours. The trailhead begins ~ 3 km from the 2nd put-in.

Info: For current information, contact Captain Holiday's Kayak Adventure School (604) 905-2925 www.kayakwhistler.com.

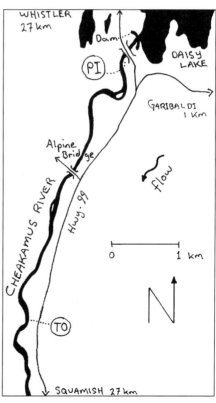

Cheakamus River (37)
Paradise Valley

Directions: From Vancouver, follow Hwy. 99 North to Squamish. From the traffic lights at Cleveland Ave., continue north ~ 10 km to a junction. Here turn Left onto Squamish Valley Rd (across Hwy. 99 from the Alice Lake Prov. Park turnoff). From Whistler, follow Hwy. 99 South until you reach Squamish Valley Rd. ~ 10 km before Squamish.

To Take-Out:
- Drive Squamish Valley Rd. ~ 3.5 km, passing a hydro-electric station, until you reach Sunwolf Outdoor Centre beside the Cheakamus. Check with the management that it is okay to park. There is a small rapid, visible from the bridge, just past this take-out. You can run it then walk back along the river's left bank.
- Cross the bridge over the Cheakamus and take a Right at the immediate **Y**. Drive ~ 3 km, passing the North Vancouver Outdoor School, until you reach the first bridge crossing the Cheakamus.

To Put-In:
- Continue driving north. The pavement ends ~ 2 km past the bridge. ~ 1 km past that, where the river is visible from the road, you will find a small dirt road on the Left. This put-in is not often used.
- If you want to run the only Class III rapid within the run, then drive ~ 2 km further to the Jack Webster bridge over Culliton Creek, then continue ~ 1.5 km to the end of the road.

Character: Scenic, small waves, small to medium volume. Great character for learning.

Considerations: Watch for log jams on this braided river.

Season: The summer months are best, but it is possible year-round, particularly after fall and winter rains.

Class: II with a II+ to III- drop at Culliton Creek.

Length of Run: ~ 10.5 km for the full run.

Shuttle: ~ 10.5 km for the full run.

cms

80
60
40
20
0

J F M A M J J A S O N D

Camping: Alice Lake Provincial Park campground. $18.50 per site. ~ 10 km north of the Cleveland Ave. lights in Squamish.

Free Camping:
▲ Small site at the 1st put-in.
▲ At Culliton Creek there are some sweet walk-in sites over the creek's canyon. Park near Jack Webster bridge and hike a short way up the North side of the creek. The sites are before you reach the railway tracks.
▲ Nice sites beside the river at the 2nd take-out bridge.
▲ Look for sites along the Cheakamus on both sides of the road. If it doesn't say private property, it probably isn't.

Lodgings:
✔ Squamish Visitor Info (604) 892-9244, email:
information@squamishchamber.bc.ca
www.squamishchamber.bc.ca
✔ Sunwolf Outdoor Centre at the take-out. Give them reason to continue to like kayakers! (604) 898-1537.

Food & Drink: Groceries, restaurants and pubs are in Squamish.

Other Activities: View eagles in the area that bills itself as the eagle capital of the world. Winter is the best time.

Info: For current information, contact Captain Holiday's Kayak Adventure School (604) 905-2925 www.kayakwhistler.com.

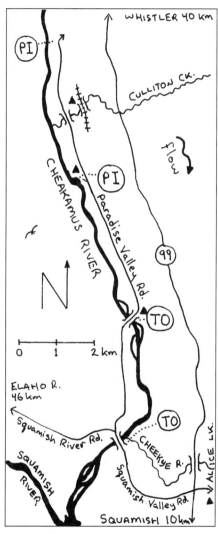

Elaho and Squamish (38) Rivers

Directions: From Vancouver, follow Hwy. 99 North to Squamish. From the traffic lights at Cleveland Ave., continue north ~ 10 km to a junction. Here turn Left onto Squamish Valley Rd (across Hwy. 99 from the Alice Lake Prov. Park turnoff). From Whistler, follow Hwy. 99 South until you reach Squamish Valley Rd. ~ 10 km before Squamish.

To Take-Out:

- For the take-out for the whole run or the Squamish run, drive along Squamish Valley Rd. ~ 3.5 kilometers until you cross the Cheakamus river. Immediately after the bridge stay Left at the **Y**. You will be on Squamish River Rd. Travel ~ 18.3 km along paved road until you reach a group of signs - one says 'No Restrictions' but be very careful of logging traffic. Continue on this logging road (now Squamish Main) ~ 17.5 km until you pass a raised water tank hidden in the branches on the Right. Just past this on the Left is a small road to pull into.

- For the Elaho run take-out, and the Squamish put-in, continue up the logging road ~ 9.2 km until you reach an intersection with Elaho Main and a bridge that spans the Squamish. Drive ~ 1 km along Elaho Main and you will see a short road on the Left that leads to the river. Have a look here across the river at the remains of an old wooden bridge. Know this spot because when you are paddling you will have to find it. To do so, as the valley broadens, follow the smaller branch to the far Left when the river braids. If you take the wrong branch you will float on by the take-out.

Boulder garden on the Elaho

To Put-In:

✦ For the Squamish put-in see the 2nd take-out.

✦ For the Elaho put-in drive ~ 2.8 km further until you see a steep, short path on the Left that leads to a treed beach. Just beyond this is a large pull-out with room for 4 - 5 cars. Pull well in so that logging traffic can still use the pull-out. Only 20 m beyond, on the right, is more parking. You will know if you have passed this when you soon come to a bridge over the Elaho.

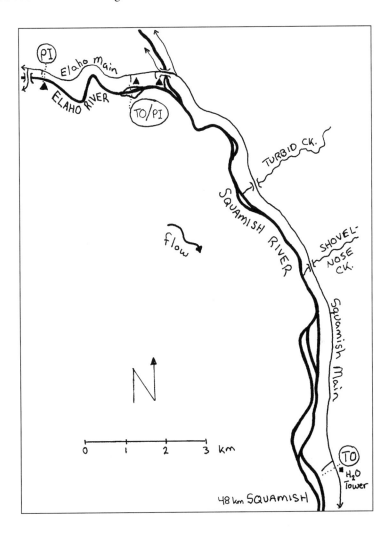

Character: Large volume rivers. Ice cold. They contain one boulder garden on the Elaho, some rock or hole gardens, and braids. On the Elaho, visible from the road, is an abrupt right-angle turn against a big, sheer headwall that may cause difficulty in big water. Some surfing and boofing depending on water level.

86

Considerations: Watch for sweepers and log jams. Water levels can rise quickly and greatly with heavy rainfall.

Season: Spring to fall, but ample rainfall at any time can allow for a paddle. A hot, clear day in September is best because you have the courage to play in the icy water, you can enjoy the glaciers and waterfalls that tower over you, and the rivers are not pushy.

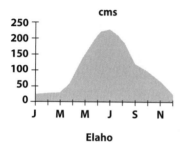

Elaho

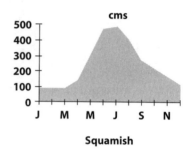

Squamish

Class: III, but you don't want to swim. Strong boil lines in high water.

Length of Run: Total: 11 km. Elaho: ~ 3 km. Squamish: ~ 8 km.

Shuttle: Total: 13 km.

Camping: Alice Lake Provincial Park campground. $18.50 per site. ~ 10 km north of the Cleveland Ave. lights in Squamish.

Free Camping:
▲ There are free sites all along both rivers; however, the put-in and the take-out for the Elaho have decent enough sites for their convenience. You just have to be aware that other kayakers may be along at any time.
▲ Nice sites on the south-west side of the bridge over the Squamish.

Lodgings: Squamish Visitor Info (604) 892-9244
email: information@squamishchamber.bc.ca   www.squamishchamber.bc.ca

Food & Drink: Groceries, restaurants and pubs are in Squamish.

Other Activities: Squamish has some excellent coastal mountain biking. Call Tantalus (604) 898-2588.

Mamquam River ㊴

Directions: From points north, follow Hwy. 99 South to Squamish. From Vancouver, follow Hwy. 99 North towards Squamish. South of Squamish, just south of the Stawamus River bridge, is the turn off to Stawamus Chief Provincial Park. It is here that climbers of the Chief park. Pass the parking lot and drive along Mamquam FS Rd. ~ 3.5 km to a large sign indicating Mamquam River Access. Continue

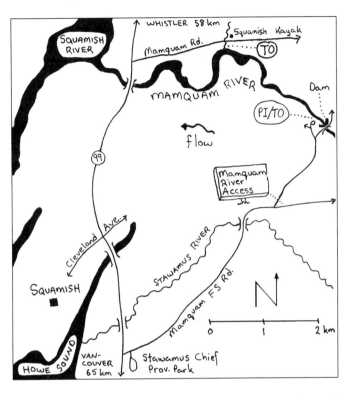

another 1.5 km, then, just past where a private road bears right to cross the dam, descend a steep gravel road to the parking lot (stay Right at the **Y**).

To Take-Out:

- ✦ This run is about paddling and walking. Walk downriver ~ 350 m to a gravel bar beside a nice wave. If you don't want the last couple of waves, you can take-out below the parking lot.
- ✦ It is possible to continue downstream, on Class II and I water. You can take-out at Squamish Kayak. Return to Hwy. 99, drive north and cross the Mamquam. In a short distance, turn Right onto Mamquam Rd. In ~ 1.5 km you will come to the shop beside Mashiter Creek.

To Put-In: You can put in anywhere, but to maximize your distance, walk ~ 350 m upriver to below the dam.

Character: Short and bone-chillin' cold. This run is ideal for practicing anything except river running - that would take about 1 minute. There is a slalom course set up, and a variety of features.

Considerations: Not much to hide here, you can see the whole run.

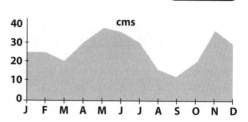

cms

J F M A M J J A S O N D

Season: Spring melt to early August. Again in the fall if it rains.

Class: III. II and I to the 2nd take-out.

Length of Run: ~ 700 m. Seconds to hours, depending on play time.

Shuttle: Depends on how far you want to walk.

Camping: Alice Lake Provincial Park campground. $18.50 per site. ~ 10 km north of the Cleveland Ave. lights in Squamish.

Free Camping:
▲ Free camping is difficult to find in the growing town of Squamish. If you find a site without a sign saying 'No Camping', try it.
▲ The Cheakamus River has many free sites beside it. Please refer to the section on the Cheakamus: Paradise Valley.

Lodgings: Squamish Visitor Info (604) 892-9244
email: information@squamishchamber.bc.ca   www.squamishchamber.bc.ca

Food & Drink: Groceries, restaurants and pubs are in Squamish.

Other Activities: Squamish is world famous for its rock climbing. Contact Climb On (604) 892-2243 or Vertical Reality (604) 892-8248.

Info: Sea to Sky Kayaking School (Squamish Kayak) (604) 898-5498 can let you know about levels, road access and downstream take-outs.

Camera-shy

Skookumchuck Narrows
(Sechelt Rapids)

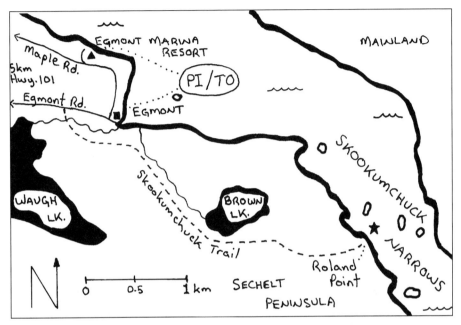

Directions: From Vancouver, follow Hwy. 1 West to Horseshoe Bay ferry terminal. Catch a 1 hour ride to Langdale (Sunshine Coast) on the Sechelt Peninsula. From there, follow Hwy. 101 to Egmont Rd. which is ~ 1.5 hours away.

To Take-Out & Put-In:
- ↕ Drive along Egmont Rd. ~ 6 km to the government wharf in Egmont. This is the closest put-in / take-out. From here the Narrows are about a 3 km flatwater paddle. If you don't paddle at slack water it will seem a lot further.
- ↕ Before the government wharf, turn Left onto Maple Rd. Drive less than 1 km to the turnoff to Egmont Marina Resort with its wharf. From here to Skookumchuck is ~ 4 km of flatwater.

Character: There are smaller waves near the islands by the mainland, but the primary wave is beside Roland Point, off the peninsula. Depending on tide and time, Skookumchuck can be anything from flat at slack tide to a fast, monstrous foam pile at flood. At points in between, the most amazing wave in this book can be found. It is wide enough for you, all your friends, and the horses they rode in on. The bigger the wave, the bigger the associated wave train, boils and eddy lines.

Considerations: Don't swim unless your fondness for swimming is all-consuming. Once you leave the confines of your boat you are at the mercy of the current which won't take you near shore for maybe an hour. And you can bet your friends aren't going to chase you. One way to avoid this is to ensure you have a good roll. Another way is to avoid the far end of the wave, which is furthest from shore and its eddy. Yet another way is to get off the sucker before it gets bigger than your abilities.

Season: All year if the rising tidal current is at least 5 knots. Anything less will not create a wave. It's best over 10 knots (it gets up to 15 knots!). You must also ensure that the rising tide occurs during the daylight, although in the summer it can be pleasant enough to paddle at night with celestial stars above and phosphorescent stars below. August and September usually offer the best alignment of all the essential elements.

Class: I to V depending on tidal difference and current.

Length of Run: If no one is waiting, as long as you want.

Shuttle: ~ 3 to 4 km of flatwater paddling.

Camping: Egmont Marina Resort has a campground beside the water. Hot showers and toilets.

A glorious moment of solitude

Free Camping:
▲ Camping is available on the various islands in the narrows. Bring everything, including water.
▲ Across from Roland Point on the mainland is a beach. Beware of private property in the area.

Lodgings:
✔ Egmont Marina Resort 1 800 626-0599, email: egmont_marina@sunshine.net
✔ Sechelt Visitor Info (604) 885-0662, email: sechelt_chamber@sunshine.net
www.thesunshinecoast.com/secheltchamber

Food & Drink: A restaurant and pub are at Egmont Marina Resort. Groceries can be found in Egmont. Full facilities are available at Sechelt.

Other Activities: Hike to and view the rapids from shore. From Egmont Rd., just west of Egmont, is a BC Parks trail that takes ~ 30 minutes to walk. It takes you right to Roland Point where the biggest wave is.

Info: Perhaps the most difficult aspect of running the Sechelt Rapids is understanding when to. You will need **current** and **tide information** to know what days the current is strong enough to create waves (which depends on tidal differences), and when the current is running for a particular day. The calculations can be quite involved so it is best to order a copy of the Canadian Hydrographic Service's Canadian Tide and Current Tables, Vol. 5: Juan de Fuca and Georgia Strait, which is updated annually in November and sells for $6.50. This can be obtained from a number of nautical shops on the coast, or through the Institute of Ocean Sciences (250) 363-6358. The Institute will also answer questions if you only want information about a specific day.

Information for **ferry schedules** can be obtained by calling: 1 888 BCFERRY (223-3779) (within BC) or (250) 386-3431(outside BC).

Long Beach
In General

Although Vancouver Island has enough whitewater features to warrant its own book, we couldn't help but add Long Beach to this one because it is such an amazing experience.

Paradise at Chesterman Beach

Long Beach goes by many names, all which describe one magical place. Some people call the area Long Beach, but that is actually just one of the beaches. Others name the area Tofino, which is really just a town on the north end of the peninsula. Some say The West Coast of the Island, which is geographically correct, but too broad. A few people call it Pacific Rim National Park, which is a big chunk of it, and includes Long Beach, but not Tofino. And to some it is Ucluelet, which is a town on the south end of the peninsula, also not in the park. You can call it paradise if you get the weather right. Regardless of the name you give it, it is a wonderful place to learn rolling and surfing.

Directions: From Vancouver, you must catch a ferry to Vancouver Island. From northern Vancouver, depart from Horseshoe Bay terminal at the west end of Hwy. 1. This takes you to Departure Bay in Nanaimo. From southern Vancouver, depart from Tsawwassen terminal at the west end of Hwy. 17. This takes you to Duke Point just south of Nanaimo. From Nanaimo, Long Beach is 165 km. Follow Hwy. 19 North, then Hwy. 4 (Pacific Rim Hwy.) until, 105 km west of Port Alberni, you reach an obvious **T** in the road. Turn Right towards Tofino. You will first reach Wickaninnish Beach, then Long Beach, Cox Bay and finally Chesterman Beach. From the **T** to Tofino is 33 km. Ucluelet is 8 km from the **T** in the opposite direction.

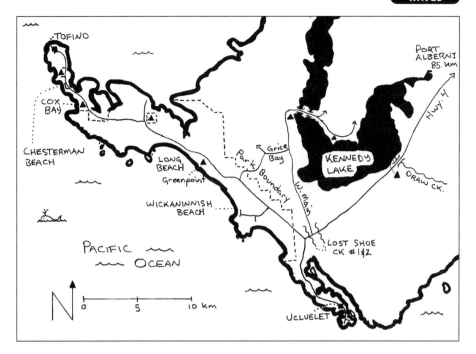

Character: Flat to abusive.

Considerations: Watch for riptide! When you first paddle out, turn around and get a visual landmark so you can gauge how much the riptide is moving you.

Season: The surf is biggest in the winter, smallest in the summer. Crowds are the inverse. Fall and spring offer nice balance.

Views: The seashore is devastating; the mountains are devastated.

Class: Varies.

Surf Information: For Wickaninnish, call the Wickaninnish Centre (250) 726-4701 and politely ask them to look out the window. For other beaches, phone Live To Surf (250) 725-4464 www.livetosurf.com and they will tell you what they know, but they can't see the beach. Wave rating billboards are at each entrance to the park.

Park Fees: Wickaninnish and Long Beach are within Pacific Rim National Park. What that means is, if you park, you pay: $3/2hrs. $8/all day $42/season

Park Information: National Park Administration (250) 726-7721.

Info Centre: (250) 726-4212 open mid-May to mid-October.

Ferry Information: 1 888 BCFERRY (223-3779) (within BC) or (250) 386-3431 (outside BC)

Getting the weather right.

Camping:

▲ National Park: Greenpoint. $18/night. Facilities except showers. Reservations 1 800 689-9025. Ask for a site above the cliff.

▲ Golf Course. Just north of Long Beach. $20/site, $25 on holidays. Outhouses.

▲ Pacific Rim Campground. Well-established, walks out onto Cox Bay surf. (250) 725-3202.

▲ Numerous more expensive sites north of the park on Mackenzie Beach and Hellesen Rds.

Free Camping:

▲ East shore of Kennedy Lake: Draw Creek. ~ 95 km from Pt. Alberni on Hwy. 4. Park where you like around the bridge unless you have a 4X4 in which case you may be able to sneak into the parking lot on the north-west side of the bridge. From there follow a 100m trail to the beach on Kennedy Lake. A tour group takes clients here 4 days a week in the summer so expect company.

▲ North shore of Kennedy Lake. For the following sites you have two approaches:

➻ From Hwy. 4, just before the **T**, take a Right onto West Main Road (it is between Lost Shoe Creek #s 1 and 2). On this good logging road travel 12 km to Clayoquot Arm Rec. Site, which is between the two bridges. Facilities include an outhouse and all the fresh water you want. A word of caution, however: it was unclear when we were there in early May 2000 whether this is a Forestry site. If it is, then fees may be charged.

➻ From the beach, ~ 3.5 km north of Wickaninnish, turn onto the landfill / fish hatchery road. Follow the orange fish arrows ~ 5.2 km until you turn Right onto Grice Bay Mainline. At ~ 2.2 km go Left onto West Main until you reach Clayoquot Arm Rec. Site. Check out the well-crafted boardwalk nearby.

▲ If this site begins charging, continue, but be warned that you should have a sturdy vehicle beyond the second bridge. Go ~ 1.5 km to a fork and take a Right. Drive ~ 4 km to a small pullout with a trail to the lake. There is plenty of flat ground, some sand, a marshy shore. ~ 0.4 km further is a site squeezed between the road and lake. The potential for other sites along the lake and elsewhere is as big as your imagination and stamina.

Lodgings: There are numerous B&Bs, hotels and resorts in Tofino and Ucluelet.
✔ Tofino Visitor Info (250) 725-3414, email: tofino@island.net
✔ Ucluelet Visitor Info (250) 726-4641, email: ucoc@ucluelet.com
✔ Hostelling International is at 81 West St. in Tofino (250) 725-3442.

Food & Drink: Grocery stores, restaurants and pubs are in Ucluelet and Tofino.

Other Activities: *In the park there are plenty of hikes, whale watching, fishing, beachcombing, surfing and all the other delights associated with the ocean. *Cathedral Grove, beside the road between Parksville and Port Alberni, is worth a quick stop if you have never seen an old-growth temperate rainforest. *Kennedy River rapids, also beside Hwy. 4, is worth scouting if only for the pleasure of scrambling beside a beautiful river (Class I - VI).

Other: Bring plenty of dry warm clothes. Did we mention plenty?

Getting the weather right again. Paradise at Long Beach

Long Beach's Beaches ㊶

Wickaninnish Beach

Directions: Off Hwy. 4 towards Tofino, ~ 3.8 km inside the park boundary, turn Left at the obvious sign. At the end of the road turn into the parking lot on your Right. Beach access points are marked **A - E**. **E** gives you the best vantage for scouting the ocean left and right.

Facilities: Toilets, picnic tables, changing stalls, cold-water sinks. An outdoor fresh water tap is at **A**. No showers. No beach fires.

Food & Drink: Wickaninnish Restaurant. Don't expect a cheap greasy spoon.

Surf Info: Wickaninnish Centre (250) 726-4701. Remember to ask politely as giving out surf info is not their main concern.

Long Beach

Directions: To get to this beach, which is inside the park, there are two accesses:
- The main parking lot is across from the airport off Hwy. 4. Follow the signs. It is ~ 15 km within the park from the South. Facilities include toilets, sinks, picnic tables, fresh water showers. No fires.
- 0.5 km further North on Hwy. 4 is another parking lot. There is no sign. This is our preferred lot because it is the only one where you can watch the surf from your vehicle. This is important on miserable days when you need all the comforts you can create. Facilities include toilets, cold-water sinks and fresh, cold-water showers.

Cox Bay (and Chesterman Beach)

Directions: Cox is the first bay after you leave the North end of the park. It is a residential area, with some resorts. There are 4 beach accesses, none of which has facilities, but all of which allow beach fires until 11pm:
- Pacific Rim campground off Hwy. 4. At the end of the short road turn Left into a small parking lot. A 300 m trail takes you to the beach.
- Further North on Hwy. 4, turn Left onto Chesterman Beach Road. 100 m along there is parking on the Right and access on the Left.
- Continue along Chesterman 0.5 km to a parking lot and access which are on the Left.
- Still further, where Chesterman, Osprey Lane and Lynn Rd. all meet, is another parking lot and access.

Englishman River Falls (42)

Englishman River Falls are just that, falls. The first one will likely kill you, the second is highly runnable. There is no associated river run, but it is so close to the highway between the west and east coasts of Vancouver Island that it is worth checking out. This is also a great place to rinse your salty gear on your return from Long Beach.

Directions: From Vancouver, you must catch a ferry to Vancouver Island. From northern Vancouver, depart from Horseshoe Bay terminal at the west end of Hwy. 1. This takes you to Departure Bay in Nanaimo. From southern Vancouver, depart from Tsawwassen terminal at the west end of Hwy. 17. This takes you to Duke Point just south of Nanaimo. From Nanaimo follow Hwy. 19 North and Hwy. 4 towards Long Beach (Tofino). About 3 km after you turn off Hwy. 19 onto Hwy. 4, turn Left onto Errington Rd. Follow the signs to the provincial park 9 km away. From Long Beach look for Errington Rd. ~ 3 km before you reach Hwy. 19.

To Put-In: Once inside the park, pass the campground and park in the near end of the day-use parking lot. This is the shortest route to the lower falls. Once at the footbridge, scramble up the trail on river right and down the small cliff to the water.

To Take-Out: From the footbridge find the path downriver on river right.

Character: Quick, vertical.

Considerations: Use the rock just to river right of center at the top of the 25 foot falls as your gauge. If it is sticking its nose out of the water you are probably OK to drop. A

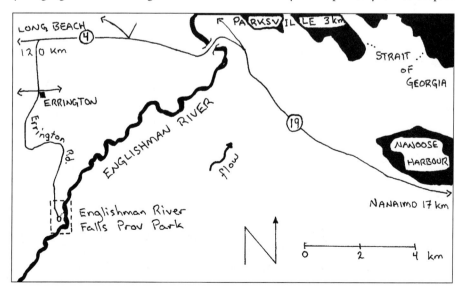

submerged rock means the landing can be grabby to the point of not letting go. Too low is too low - you decide! Run on river left; river right requires elbow pads.

Season: All year except the late summer months until the fall rains begin.

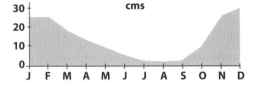

Class: Tough to grade a vertical drop, but the higher the water level, the more skill required to extricate yourself from the bottom. Definitely IV and up.

Camping:
▲ The BC Parks campground is $15/site. It has firewood, outhouses and water taps.
▲ Tranquillity Woods is a private campground outside the park. It is $12/site.

Lodgings: Parksville Visitor Info (250) 248-3613, email: info@chamber.parksville.bc.ca www.chamber.parksville.bc.ca

Food & Drink: Restaurants, pubs and grocery stores are in Parksville.

Other Activities: The hike around both falls is short and nearby. It gives you the chance to decide if you are game for the upper falls ☺.

High water - too high!

Chilko River ㊸

This is an abbreviated description of the Chilko River, a long, internationally known river that includes the legendary "White Mile" (from a movie of the same name). It has been included courtesy of Red Shred's Bike and Board Shed in Williams Lake, Cariboo Chilcotin Adventure Guides and the Cariboo Chilcotin Coast Tourism Association. We offer a brief overview here, but full details, including maps and links to water flow info, are available from Red Shred's (250) 398-7873, 955 1st Ave, Williams Lake, or on the Association's web site www.cariboocountry.org

Directions: From Vancouver, follow Hwy. 1 East to Cache Creek and then Hwy. 97 North to Williams Lake. The drive takes ~ 6 hours. From Williams Lake, follow Hwy. 20 West ~130 km until you turn south on the gravel Chilko Newton Road. This road takes you to the headwaters at Chilko Lake.

To Take-Out & Put-In: For complete details, obtain info from the above contacts. The road more or less parallels the river. Access points are where Chilko Newton Rd. swings near the river.

Character: The river is ~ 92 km long and offers a variety of Classes. The first section, Chilko Lake to Henry's Crossing, is Class I and II. It is wide and mellow. A river rafting company's campsite and launch ramp, on river Left ~ 7.5 km past Henry's Crossing, indicate the real end of this section. The second section, Henry's Crossing to Taseko Junction, is the most difficult and contains canyon features and Class I to IV+ rapids, including Bidwell Rapids and the White Mile. Here the run becomes steeper and it contains more holes, waves and rocks in the drops. The third section, Taseko Junction to Bull Canyon, is Class II to III+. This is a fun, playful run with plenty of surf waves.

Considerations: Scout Bidwell Rapids on the second section, recognizable by the increasing ferocity of the river. Get out on river Left and follow a short trail to a vantage point. Scout Siwash Bridge on the third section. This is a narrow funnel under the bridge - avoid at high water. Watch for wood debris throughout. Be careful of bears at camping, put-in and take-out sites.

Season: May to October.

Class: I to IV+.

Length of Run: ~ 92 km altogether.

Shuttle: ~ 100 km.

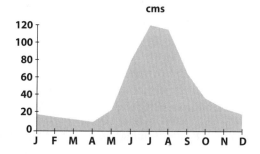

Camping:
▲ Taseko River Junction FS site at the end of the second section.
▲ Bull Canyon FS site at the end of the third section.

Free Camping: Contact Red Shred's for info on any possible free sites.

Lodgings: Williams Lake Visitor Info (250) 392-5025, email: wldc@stardate.bc.ca

Food & Drink: Williams Lake has restaurants, pubs and groceries.

Other Activities: Plenty of mountain biking in the area. Contact Red Shred's Bike and Board Shed (250) 398-7873.

Cariboo River

This is an abbreviated description of the Cariboo River, which can be divided into two sections: Upper and Lower. It has been included courtesy of Red Shred's Bike and Board Shed in Williams Lake, Cariboo Chilcotin Adventure Guides and the Cariboo Chilcotin Coast Tourism Association. We offer a brief overview here, but full details, including maps and links to water flow info, are available from Red Shred's (250) 398-7873, 955 1st Ave, Williams Lake, or on the Association's web site www.cariboocountry.org

Directions: From Vancouver, follow Hwy. 1 East to Cache Creek and then Hwy. 97 North to Williams Lake. The drive takes ~ 6 hours. ~ 15 km South of Williams Lake, turn East onto Horsefly Road. In a short distance, turn Left onto Likely Rd. and drive ~ 80 km to the town of Likely. There is a popular surf spot on the Quesnel River below Likely Bridge.

<u>Lower Section</u> (Keithley Creek Rd. Bridge to Quesnel Forks)

To Take-Out: From Likely, drive to the old ghost town of Quesnel Forks. Contact Red Shred's for further details.

To Put-In: Return to Likely, then continue North out of Likely. The main road turns to gravel, and then crosses the Cariboo River at Keithley Creek Rd. Bridge in ~ 7 km.
🔱 The north bank (steep) of the river is the put-in (and the take-out for the Upper section).
🔱 A better put-in (/take-out) is ~ 1.5 km downstream. After crossing the bridge, take the first Left which is Pearson Rd. Continue a short distance and take a spur road that heads down to the river (~ 200 m) to parking and a beach.

Character: Large volume, one narrow canyon, standing waves, boulders. Run the center of the river.

Considerations: Watch for wood debris.

Season: May to October.

Class: II to III. High water can be IV.

Length of Run: ~ 12 km.

Shuttle: Check with Red Shred's, but it is more than 12 km.

Upper Section (Cariboo Falls to Keithley Creek Rd. Bridge)

To Take-Out: Please refer to the instructions for To Put-In for Lower Section.

To Put-In: From the Keithley Creek Rd. Bridge, continue north a short distance and turn Right onto Keithley Creek Rd. At the 15 km marker, turn Right onto an old logging road and drive through a cut-block for a short distance. As the road comes close to the river, it turns left and heads upstream to the fish ladder at Cariboo Falls. At this point you will likely encounter a locked gate. If it is locked, walk a short distance to a rock cairn that marks a trail down to the put-in **below** the Falls.

Character: Large volume, big holes, drops, giant waves. The web site or Red Shred's can give you a detailed description.

Considerations: Watch out for wood debris.

Season: May to October.

Class: IV to IV+.

Length of Run: ~ 10 km.

Shuttle: ~ 10 - 12 km depending on take-out.

Camping & Free Camping: Contact Red Shred's or Visitor Info.

Lodgings: Williams Lake Visitor Info (250) 392-5025, email: wldc@stardate.bc.ca

Food & Drink: Williams Lake has restaurants, pubs and groceries.

Other Activities: Check out historic sites associated with the Cariboo Gold Rush all along the river. Contact Red Shred's or Visitor Info.

Glossary
of terms used in this book

n = noun; v = verb; adj = adjective [some words are more than one]

Boil (n)   - a welling up of water below a rapid or waterfall; found in large-volume water.

Bony (adj)   - describes shallow water with many rocks showing.

Boof (v)   - to use a smooth rock in the river as a jump.

Boulder garden (n)   - a section of river with many boulders to maneuver around.

Braided (adj)   - describes a river that divides repeatedly into two or more channels.

Broach (v)   - to be stuck sideways between an obstacle (rock) and the current.

Busy (adj)   - describes active water that requires maneuvering.

Chute (n)   - a (usually short) navigable channel in a drop.

Continuous (adj)   - describes whitewater without flat spots.

Drop (n)   - a (usually short) feature in which the river descends quickly. Waterfalls are big drops.

Eddy (n)   - an area of (relatively) calm water beside or within the main current. It is formed by a protrusion into the river (like a bend), or a boulder in the river, that causes the current to reverse. Very useful for boat-scouting.

Eddy Line (n)   - the seam between the eddy and the main current.

Flip (v)   - to capsize your kayak while you are still in it. (first half of a roll)

Headwall (n)   - a cliff face that abruptly turns a river 90°.

Hole (n)   - turbulent water that flows back on itself, created by and downstream of a submerged rock or other obstacle.

Hole garden (n)   - a section of river with many holes to maneuver around.

House rock (n)   - a massive boulder in a river.

Keeper (n)   - a large hole that won't let you go.

Line (n)   - a navigable path through whitewater, as in: "I missed my line".

Logjam (n)   - a pile of wood that the current has gathered, usually at a bend or at the top of an island. Water flows through and beneath it, as might you. Very dangerous.

Pool-drop (adj)   - describes a river with a series of drops that fall into calm pools.

Portage (v)   - to carry your boat over land around a difficult stretch of whitewater. In Canada it is pronounced *portawwge*.

Pounding (adj)   - as a hammer is to a nail, so this water is to you.

Put-in (n)   - where you put your boat in the water at the top of a run.

Riffles (n)   - small, inconsequential waves.

River left (n)   - the left when you are facing downstream.

River right (n)   - the right when you are facing downstream.

Rock garden (n)   - a section of river that has many visible rocks.

Roll (v)   - after flipping, this is the act of righting your boat with you still in it. Also called 'Eskimo roll'.

Scout (v)   - stopping above a drop or difficult section of whitewater to find your line. Can be done from shore (for more difficult features) or from your boat.

Squirrelly (adj)   - describes water that swirls and is unpredictable. Usually after big drops and in steep canyons.

Surf (v)   - to ride a wave facing upstream.

Sweeper (n)   - a tree or branch sticking out from shore that is just above or below the water surface. Very dangerous.

Swim (v)   - when you have failed to roll, this is your last option. Remember to grab your boat and paddle.

Take-out (n) - where you take your boat out of the water at the end of a run.

Technical (adj) - describes whitewater that requires precise maneuvering.

Wave Train (n) - a series of waves, one after another.

Weir (n) - a man-made or natural dam-like structure that crosses the width of a river. Unlike a dam, water flows over it. Potentially dangerous keepers behind.

Bridge River Coliseum

Little Things to Think About

During the research for this book we learned a few things beyond our intentions. We thought we would share these with you, at no extra cost!

Items to Bring
- extra keys
- duct tape (of course)
- utility tool (ie. Leatherman, Gerber)
- ear plugs (for when you are lucky
enough to share a campsite with a high school graduating class)
- hide-a-key
- spare tire and jack
- guidebook (optional)

Actions to Remember
- if using your vehicle as a tarp anchor, be sure to untie the tarp before driving away from the site.
- never leave anything on the bumper, fender or roof of your vehicle.
- be aware of fire closures where you are camping.
- when looking for put-ins, take-outs, campsites, etc. on logging roads do not pause or stop in blindspots. The logging truck drivers know the roads and haul ass.
- at Forestry sites you are charged per vehicle. However, a second is permitted free if used as a commuter. If you take the time to explain to the attendant that your second vehicle is an unfortunate evil necessary for kayak shuttles, you may only have to pay for one.
- always ask the drivers if they have their keys.
- carry an extra paddle in your group.
- if you have a question, ask it.

Recommended Reading

Backroad Mapbook, volumes I, II, III and IV by Mussio Ventures

"BC Min. of Forests Recreation Maps" available from Government Agents, Visitor Info Centres, FS District Offices, vendors of FS camping passes and Canadian Cartographics Ltd. (887) 524-3337 (toll free) www.canmap.com

High Country Hiking: A Guide to Trails in the Kamloops Area by Charles Bruce

"Super, Natural British Columbia Accommodations Guide" by Tourism British Columbia 1 800 435-5622, www.HelloBC.com

Whistler Outdoors Guide by Jack Christie

Whitewater Trips for Kayakers, Canoeists and Rafters on Vancouver Island by Betty Pratt-Johnson

Environment Canada's River Level Website: Link through www.kayakwhistler.com

About the Authors

When we first started telling people about our summer project - writing a whitewater kayaking guide book - we received a variety of responses, including: "Huh?", "Wow, great!", "Oh, my sister sea kayaks around Victoria", "It's about time someone did that", "I'd like to try sea kayaking", and our favorite, "You call that work? Work isn't supposed to be fun". Some of these sentiments inspired us, some deflated us. All the comments about sea kayaking got us thinking that maybe there is a larger market for a sea kayaking guide book, but our minds were made up about the whitewater (and besides, we don't own sea kayaks).

We have both always enjoyed the great outdoors that this part of the world is blessed with. Whether skiing, snowboarding, rock climbing, hiking, mountain biking, sea kayaking, canoeing or whitewater kayaking, we have tried to figure out ways to make a living while enjoying the lifestyle. After many years, and as many false starts, writing this book was the first feasible idea we came up with.

And to put to rest those minds that have concerned themselves with such thoughts - we assure you no fun was had doing this project!

Steve Crowe

Originally from Kamloops, Steve has ventured far and wide, always to return to the uncrowded, dry, rolling landscape of BC's southern Interior. As a forest fire fighter, he spent many summers wistfully looking at rivers from helicopters until he snapped at the end of the 1999 season. It was then that he decided that guaranteed income was far less rewarding than the uncertainty of self-employment. He's optimistic that regret is not in his future. But he hasn't burnt any bridges, nor his Bachelor of Education degree, just in case.

Jim Hnatiak

After learning the hard way that Class VI rivers are a bit too challenging for a first-time paddler, Jim has been making the best of the lower numbers. His love of finding new lines through water, whether it is clinging frozen to a mountainside or roaring through a gorge, keeps him exploring the southwest of BC, where he has spent most of his life.

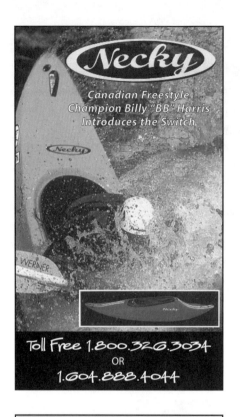

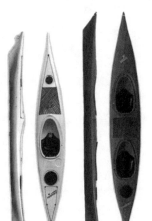